Ever wonder if there is more to leadership than learning the latest strategy for going further faster? You're not alone. In our fast-paced world of ministry leadership, it's easy to get lost in the maze of daily distraction and completely miss what God is doing all around us. Gail takes us on a journey to discover how leading from a healthy soul can make all the difference. This is a must-read for those who have a deeper longing to learn the ancient ways of attentive leadership that can keep us in sync with the work of God we all desperately want to be a part of. This is our invitation to slow down, pay attention, and listen the voice of the Spirit who will transform us from being busy leaders to ones who make a significant impact through attentive living.

– DR. BETH BACKES
Pastor, speaker, leadership coach

In today's climate of leadership, I can't think of a timelier book than *All There*, written by my friend, Dr. Gail Johnsen. My wife, Debbie, and I have ridden thousands of miles together with Gail and her husband, Darrel, on Harley Davidson motorcycles. Harley believes in genuine motor parts—parts you can count on. Today our world needs authentic, genuine leaders who take the time to stay spiritually, mentally and emotionally healthy. Authentic leaders you can count on. Leaders attentive to the needs of others. Leaders who put others first and live out true servanthood. Dr. Gail Johnsen is a proven scholar in the field of leadership. I encourage you to read this book with an open heart to make sure you are all there as you lead.

– DR. DAVE E. COLE
Northwest Ministry Network
Author of *Refocus: Creating an Outward-Focused Church Culture*

When I look back over my life, it is easy to see my blind spots. Regrets about what I should have done and didn't, or what I did and shouldn't, stand out clearly. I should have paid more attention. In my quest to lead a growing church and network, I often became easily distracted. Gail—I can see more clearly now; thanks for helping with those blind spots so I can focus on what is before me with new eyes.

– DR. DON DETRICK
Northwest Ministry Network
Author of *Growing Disciples Organically: The Jesus Method of Spiritual Formation*

It is no secret to the discerning leader—the world in which we live and minister has drastically changed. So many of those to whom we're called to bring the message of Good News in our secular society can spot the incongruities in our lives a mile away. Jesus brings peace and hope, we say, but often our frantic, anxious, rushing lives say something else. We want our being to match our doing and our saying, but how does that become a reality in an age of relentless distractions? In *All There: How Attentiveness Shapes Authentic Leadership*, Dr. Gail Johnsen puts handles on what it means to live and lead from a place of integrated wholeness where what we say comes from the overflow of our deep connection to Jesus. As her friend, I've had a front row seat and the privilege of watching Dr. Johnsen live out these powerful principles and teach them to ministry leaders for years. I couldn't be more excited that she's compiled all she's learned into book form for the benefit of the rest of us. *All There* is beautifully written, filled with personal stories and engaging anecdotes which bring color and life to her message of what it means to live a life of attentiveness and presence. Every ministry leader should read this book, starting with YOU, my friend.

– DR. JODI DETRICK

Author of *The Jesus-Hearted Woman: 10 Leadership Qualities for Enduring & Endearing Influence*

All There will change your life and ministry! Gail Johnsen unpacks the practice of attentive listening in a way that opens the soul care we all long for and desperately need. This beautiful exchange allows us to minister from a place of abundance instead of emptiness, just as God designed it to be. I wholeheartedly encourage you to journey through this book and experience your leadership transformed by the shift of your soul.

– CHERYL JAMISON

Executive Team Member, Eastridge Church

Truly an incredible book! Every pastor and leader needs to read and digest this book. We get caught in the fuscous trap of working for God and not walking with God. Listening seems counterproductive. Our souls become dysfunctional in a day where silence is rare. Dr. Johnsen does an outstanding job helping leaders listen. Pause. Be Attentive!

– DR. TROY H. JONES

Lead Pastor, New Life Church, Renton, WA

Author of *Recalibrate Your Church: How Your Church Can Reach Its Full Kingdom Impact*

So good, so needed. I feel as though I've had a drink of cool water from every chapter. This is a summons to reshape how you spend yourself. As a minister, I am taking notes. And sitting a while.

– DR. ROSEMARIE KOWALSKI
Strategic Missional Leader
Author of *What Made Them Think They Could? Women in Early Pentecostal Missions*

If we could pass this on to our people in the church, we would transform what discipleship is all about. The implications for the Church at large is incredible. I am so excited about this book! *All There* book is worth your time!

– DR. KIM MARTINEZ
Pastor and Leadership Consultant

Even to produce this remarkable book on attentiveness required exercising the very spiritual disciplines the author advocates—the kind of attention to God, self, and others that results in personal, interpersonal, and divine interactions of deep value and eternal worth. It was my honor not only to serve as Dr. Johnsen's project coordinator during her doctoral work, but also her editor on this volume, and I can testify to her authentic life that resulted in such a book. *All There* isn't just another leadership book; it is a timely sacred space for 2020 when innumerable crises and uncertainties threaten to derail us. Attend to it as a place of solace, reflection, and encouragement for this moment of living in Christ's yoke—this place of rest, empowerment, direction, and love.

– DR. LOIS E. OLENA
Associate Professor (ret.), AGTS
Springfield, Missouri
Former Executive Director, Society for Pentecostal Studies
Author of *Stanley Horton: Shaper of Pentecostal Theology*

When I first met Gail, I knew she was a leader to follow—an authentic soul. Her book, *All There,* is an impassioned call for every leader to lean in and listen, love a lost world so profoundly that the idea of being right wanes in light of his great love, and allow brokenness to find its redemptive healing place in our lives and our world. You will notice quickly that Gail's thoughts and research are deeply rooted in Scripture and from a place of personal experience—her spiritual formation. I read every word, and it has already made me a more intentional follower of Jesus. *All There* is a much-needed conversation for today's leaders.

– LISA POTTER
Executive Director of Women Who Lead

Dr. Gail Johnsen cares well for her soul … and will help you care better for yours! In her easy-to-read style, her beautifully written book will help you become a healthier leader and actually enjoy ministry more. Gail will take you on an authentic journey, so don't just read this book to learn, read it to grow, because you will be challenged. I have been in her attentive leader sessions, and I am a better leader for it. You'll be glad you made the investment in time and money to read *All There: How Attentiveness Shapes Authentic Ministry!*

– DR. DONALD E. ROSS
Northwest Ministry Network Leader
Author of *Turnaround Pastor: Pathways to Save, Revive and Build Your Church*

Gail Johnsen introduces us to a dynamic form of authentic leadership based on a stance and state of alltherenes. Alltherenes is less about your ability to command attention than your willingness to pay attention, less about put on your Sunday best, don that thinking cap, and watch how "these boots are made for walking" than open up your listening ears, stretch out your hands, and take off your shoes—in the presence of another human being, you're on holy ground.

– DR. LEONARD SWEET
Best-selling Author, Professor, and Founder of PreachTheStory.com

If you are caught in a spiritual performance trap, this book will help you find your way out. Along the way, you will encounter compelling stories, timeless biblical truths, and spiritual habits for faithful living in a constantly distracted age. Gail is a ministry leader who truly practices what she preaches.

– DR. ROBERT H. WOODS
Executive Director, Christianity and Communication Studies Network
(www.theccsn.com)

All There

How Attentiveness Shapes Authentic Leadership

DR. GAIL JOHNSEN

FOREWORD BY
James T. Bradford

ALL THERE: HOW ATTENTIVENESS SHAPES AUTHENTIC LEADERSHIP

For permission requests, please address: gailjohnsen.com or gailj5701@gmail.com

ISBN 13: 978-0-578-78743-5

Cataloguing-in-Publication Data

All There: How Attentiveness Shapes Authentic Leadership by Gail Johnsen; foreword by James T. Bradford.

xxiv + 228 p.; 23 cm. Includes bibliographical references.
ISBN 13: 978-0-578-78743-5
I. Johnsen, Gail. II. Bradford, James T.
III. All There: How Attentiveness Shapes Authentic Leadership.

CALL NUMBER 2020

Printed in the United States of America 2020

Cover design: Devyn North
Printed by Sheridan

Dedication

To my amazing husband, Darrel.

Thank you for your constant encouragement to pursue God's purposes and ways in my life; for out-loving the unfinished places of my soul; and showing me how to move gracefully in the world.

How can I be anything but grateful?

Table of Contents

Foreword

It has been surprising to me how toxic vocational ministry can be to my spiritual health. Most people would not think so. "Pastor, I wish I had a job like yours, just being able to read the Bible and pray all the time." But the continual indulging of our well-intentioned drivenness can create serious spiritual and emotional slip-page in our lives. Activity for God can too easily replace intimacy with God. We may even find ourselves loving leadership more than we love Jesus. Unfortunately, our own souls become the casualties in the end.

By the time I was twenty-seven years of age, I had been the student leader of a campus ministry, finished a Ph.D., and planted a university church. Over the next couple of years that church doubled in size. It was a spiritually dynamic time. The Holy Spirit was moving, and I was personally praying two hours a day. But, strangely, people started saying things to me like, "Pastor, why do you look so sad all the time?" Or, "When I pray for you, I keep feeling that the Lord wants to make you a real person." In reality, I did not know why I was feeling the way I was, and it upset me that people even noticed. As for being a 'real person,' I had no idea what that was about, which frustrated me even more.

Ultimately all of that culminated in a transformational six-month journey with the Lord that meant cutting back on speaking ministry outside of the church and having a 'date' with God every Saturday night. I was single at the time and working eighty hours a week. I certainly needed to physically slow down and emotionally restore, but I especially needed to reframe the spiritual center out of which I was ministering to others.

During that time, I heard about two couples who had divorced after twenty-five years of marriage. Once the last child had left home, they looked at each other and realized that they were living with a stranger. I sensed that the Lord was saying to me, "That's just like you and me. Sure, you pray two hours a day, but all we do is talk about the kids. It's like we don't know each other any more."

Those dates with God—during which it seemed out of bounds to pray about the church—began to restore me. It alarms me now that, in the end, it took me six months to recover the joy that ministry activism had eroded. Surprisingly, that new joy was not centered in having a church that had just doubled in size, but in simply refocusing on being with Jesus. And as 'unproductive' as some of those dates with God felt, He began to reshape me as a 'real person'—not as a successful pastor, but simply as His treasure with nothing to prove. I also noticed that public ministry began feeling more effortless.

That is why I so resonate with the journey that Gail Johnsen takes us on in *All There.* We dare not lose our own souls in the pursuit of God's call. But be warned: this book is not about quick fixes. It is, instead, about who and what we pay attention to. The spiritual disciplines can no longer be an end in and of themselves. They are simply a means to a greater end, the freedom of surrender as opposed to the pressure of always having to try harder. It is the place of striving less and responding more to God's invitation to become a part of what He is already doing.

In Gail's own words, "I failed to realize that pushing and shoving and doing all the 'right things' does not bring life to your soul—ever." Instead, we can choose a different and a better way. In the words of the Apostle Paul, "God … has called you into fellowship with His Son, Jesus Christ" (1 Cor 1:9). There we start, and there we end. So, read with an open and a hungry heart.

Dr. James T. Bradford
Lead Pastor,
Central Assembly, Springfield, Missouri

Introduction: An Invitation to Wholeness

"We have long ago dispensed with the notion that
leadership is a set of competencies to be learned
or just so many boxes to be checked. Admitting instead
that, as Warren Bennis writes, it is the 'integrated human being'
among us—the individuated, mature, and developing man
or woman—who is most fit for the task of leadership,
we must look more carefully at the role the inner life plays
in becoming that person."[1]

"The way to life—to God—is vigorous and requires
your total attention" (Luke 13:23, MSG).

"So, what is God up to in your life?" asked Jodi Detrick, my iron-sharpening friend. Whenever possible, Jodi and I would grab a few stolen moments and catch up on life and ministry over a cup of coffee. As so often happened, our time together began with this question. This time there was a pause in my response. My mind sifted through the unspoken realities of my heart.

"I don't know," I honestly confided. "But God is up to something."

As soon as I said it, this stirring somehow became real: God *was* doing something in my life. I didn't know what that was, and although this stirring felt unfamiliar, I sensed God was speaking, and I needed to pay attention.

A week later, somewhere in the side streets of my soul came a whisper: "There has to be more." Surprised and a little embarrassed by the voice, I wanted to brush it off, but the whisper wouldn't go away. An unexplainable longing had settled into my soul. It actually felt more like an ache. It was baffling to experience such longing this far into my Christian journey and after thirty years of full-time vocational ministry.

I quickly made a spiritual to do checklist to figure out how this breach occurred. Bible reading? Somewhat consistent … check. Prayer? Arrows shot up to heaven mostly on the run (because I was so busy) … check. Ministry? Unbridled activity and relentless obligations … check. If I were honest: exhausted, discouraged, and overwhelmed … check. I remembered reading in Matthew 11:28 when Jesus said, "My yoke is easy and my burden is light"[2] and thinking, it sure doesn't feel that way.

Not long afterward, in yet another unguarded moment, I blurted out loud, "If I do not encounter Jesus in a real way, I am going to die!" There it was: my soul's cry. No more denial. No more hiding behind church leadership. No more using busyness as a distraction. I powerfully experienced the Psalmist's sigh: "My soul yearns, even faints, for the courts of the Lord; My heart and my flesh cry out for the living God" (Ps 84:2).

How does one's soul lose life-giving connection in the midst of spiritual leadership? I had been in full-time vocational ministry for thirty years, yet I thought of Jesus saying to me as He did to Philip, "Don't you know me, Gail, even after I have been among you such a long time?" (John 14:9).

Somewhere in the flurry of activity, the part of me that connected with God on the deepest level had been left behind. My soul was desperate for an authentic encounter with God that did not include me trying to manipulate, manufacture, or pretend that encounter. What I failed to realize is that pushing and shoving and doing all the 'right' things does not bring life to your soul—ever.

Trying to achieve the spiritual life by our tireless efforts must have been what the prophet Jeremiah meant when he wrote, "They have forsaken me, the spring of living water, and have dug their own cisterns, broken cisterns that cannot hold water" (2:13). My soul was screaming, "Water! Water!" And what did I do? I grabbed a shovel of busyness, competence, and achievement, trying to dig my own well, thinking I could stave off my thirst. But it didn't work. The flurry of my ministry activity could no longer appease my restless heart. All I was left with was a hectic schedule and a disintegrated soul.

Perhaps the spiritual life is less about striving
and more about
noticing invitations.

Surprisingly, I did not hear the accusing voice I had heard so often, "You need to try harder." When in reality, my restless soul was a sign of God's gracious activity. I was not the one producing all this; I was the one being acted upon. My longing for something more did not come by my own efforts but by way of invitation. Perhaps the spiritual life is less about striving and more about noticing invitations.

In that moment, everything changed. I knew I needed to let go of the death grip I had on trying to achieve the spiritual life and all the busyness surrounding that. I felt stuck. I knew there was more. I felt like Abraham. God was calling me to a place where I had never been. I didn't know how I was to get there or how I would know when I had arrived. I did not know what life looked like outside all my striving.

Instinctively, I knew I had to move in a different way that would keep me alive and attentive to this new work of grace. I needed a way to embrace God's real and very-near presence as an ongoing reality. I wasn't sure what that meant or how it might look. One thing was for sure: my soul was not going to settle for less.

Come to find out, my coming apart became an amazing grace.

Spiritual leadership begins, not by our ingenuity and ceaseless activity, but by first, being committed to a journey of personal wholeness.

All There is a call to a holistic way of leadership. Whatever your ministry context, the kind of authentic (integrated) leadership needed in today's secular age relies heavily on the Jesus's mandate to love God with all your heart, soul, and mind, and to love your neighbor as yourself (Mark 12:29-31).

Jesus invites us to give careful attention, i.e., being "all there," to the three essential dimensions of human life: God, self, and others, and all the ways He is bringing about wholeness to those places. Jesus was not calling us to try harder to be more loving but to be attentive to the right things. Ultimately, our ongoing wholeness plays an integral part in Jesus's redemptive kingdom purposes.

Jesus was not calling us to try harder to be more loving but to be attentive to the right things.

The focus of the book asserts that spiritual leadership involves leading from a place of hearing and responding to what the Spirit has to say. Thus, the underpinnings of our leadership is to listen, i.e., to be fully present, long enough to notice what the Spirit is already doing. God, then, invites us to participate with the unique kingdom work we are given to do. This means we can have the confidence that God has already set into motion what is most needed in our leadership setting. As Ruth Haley Barton concludes, "But at the heart of spiritual leadership is the capacity to notice the activity of God so we can join him in it."[3]

Leading well in a culture of distraction will require intentional rhythms and practices that train our souls to attentiveness. As we are confronted with cultural realities, such as secularism and distraction, and the challenge of leading others, our ability to live authentically will become more and more essential.

This leadership book is unique in examining the role that attentiveness plays as the basis for authentic ministry leadership.

In chapter 1, we examine the processes that brought me to this distance place in the midst of leadership. I identify three (although there are more) contributing factors that contribute to disintegration in ministry.

In chapters 2-3, we consider that spiritual leadership involves leading from a place of hearing and responding to what the Spirit has to say. Thus, our first responsibility as a leader is not to make something happen, but to listen and respond to what we hear, no matter how disruptive it seems. Ultimately, listening gives us the courage to act.

In chapter 4, we examine the loss of attentiveness in our culture and the lengths our culture will go to keep us scattered and distracted. As leaders, were not exempt from this crisis of attention. The cost of our distraction is high, to our souls and to those we lead.

In chapter 5, we look at the essentialness of spiritual practices as the antidote to our distracted and disintegrated lives. Intentional, spiritual practices are our most basic tools by which we pay attention to God, to ourselves, and to those around us.

In chapters 6-8, we consider what it means to be 'all there' to God and to His gracious activity in our lives. We look at specific spiritual practices that train our hearts to stay focused, open, and responsive to the transforming Presence of Christ in us, that we might offer those we serve something real, meaningful, and life-giving.

In chapters 9 and 10, we turn our attention and practices to the hidden, interior life of the leader. Far from being antisocial or narcissistic, being present to our inner life rises as essential if we are to lead from a place of authenticity. Our personal faithfulness as leaders must include a courageous readiness look at our how life is unfolding and not assume that all of our life is as it appears. The emotional development and integrity of the leader will serve as a key differentiator in the days ahead.

In chapters 11 and 12, we conclude with the leadership dimension of remaining fully present to others. Offering loving attention to others becomes an important apologetic in our emerging culture. The reality of the gospel is most compelling when our lives reflect the reality of Christ. As we are transformed by the love of Christ, we seamlessly move in the world and relate to people through postures of kindness, empathy, and gracious conversations.

Ministry is not what it used to be. We live in an age intolerant of institutions, skeptical of formalized religion, and weary of hypocrisy by practitioners of faith. It is here where the person of the leader who can lead comfortably from a soul still in process, stumbling toward authenticity, becomes most compelling. I don't know your ministry context, but may you become that leader that is most needed in our day. May your way of being with God, yourself, and others compel others not toward you, but toward the holy work that has occurred within your soul. Ultimately, the ability to pay attention is at the heart of authentic and spiritual leadership. Being "all there" percolates to the top as an essential component of personal wholeness, life-giving leadership, and effective ministry. Perhaps that is what those we serve need the most.

Stay open.

Stay attentive.

1

I Am Not Alone

"Leadership failure is not so much a failure of ethics as it is a failure of human wholeness."[1]

Intuitively I knew that my story of disintegration was not unique. Over the last ten years, I have led many ministry leaders through a nine-month spiritual formation journey. There, I witnessed firsthand the struggles of ministry leaders to intentionally prioritize spiritual, personal, and relational well-being in the cacophony of ministry.

At the beginning of the nine-month journey, I asked participants to describe in one word, and as honestly as possible, how the spiritual life felt to them. (No 'right' or trite Sunday school answers were allowed.) In this safe environment and with formidable vulnerability, they came to describe the spiritual life as: "obligatory," "unattainable," "demanding," "empty," "going through the motions," "work," "frustrating," "trapped," "solving," "forced," "exhausting" and "the pressure to perform." Their words were stark but honest. No one ever answered, "abundant."

These were capable and competent ministry leaders who loved Jesus. They loved the Church and gave their lives in service to others. They were called, committed, and extremely gifted to lead, yet there seemed to exist a gut-level disconnect between the truths they held in their heads (and preached) and the realities of their lives. Many, unknowingly and unintentionally, were leading from a place of exhaustion, discouragement, and disillusionment; and, some, from a soul untethered from its centeredness in God.

We lead out of an overflow of who we are. If we are weary, distracted, or restless, these inner realities form the essence of our ministry. In other words, if we are experiencing disintegration, we minister from a place of disintegration.

We can have a 'successful' ministry
and yet live with a
diminished soul.

Perhaps this is what Jesus meant when he said, "What good will it be for someone to gain the whole world, yet forfeit their soul? Or what anyone give in exchange for their soul?" (Matt 16:26). Perhaps Jesus wasn't talking about losing our soul in an eternal way, but in a human way—in a present-tense kind of way. We can have a 'successful' ministry and yet live with a diminished soul. In the swirl of ministry, we can lead from a place inauthentic to who we really are, defined by what we do, be driven by who is watching, and never live fully present to those things that would bring health and wholeness to our lives.

How Did We Get This Way?

How do ministry leaders get to a place of disintegration? How does ministry create such a divided life? There are many reasons, but four stand out: (1) the prominent church growth culture, (2) our hyper-activity of working hard for God, and (3) failure to take seriously the importance of the soul. The fourth reason, (4) our culture's disposition of hurry and distraction, will be addressed in chapter 4.

Prominent Church Growth Culture

In recent decades, the emphasis of church growth and leadership has produced a raft of bestsellers with such titles as, *Ten Ways to…*; *How to Make…*; *Five Surprising Truths…*, *Nine Things You Don't…*, *Three Essential Habits…*, and so on. The unspoken message we receive is that the weight of our church's success or effective ministry revolves around our leadership capabilities and ingenuity. We presume we can find the secret to effective ministry in the next book, the next leadership conference, or the next megachurch pastor's podcast. What we really want is the silver bullet that resolves our concerns about stagnant or declining attendance, our doubts, or our lack of leadership skills. We seek practical solutions in strategy and time management, strength assessments, collaboration, teamwork, and communication. Certainly, leadership tools are valuable, but an undue reliance on strategies and methodologies often overshadows the equally essential personhood of the leader and the life of the Spirit.

The pressure to produce is constant. Hooked on outcomes, our pursuit of ministry success may become defined and applauded by tireless actions and personal proficiency. In doing so, we become less and less committed to a holistic way of life.

In addition, being the expert and being 'on' all the time—or pretending we 'have it all together'—is not only inauthentic, it is unsustainable and produces a divided life—one that is public and one that is private. Eventually, our personal lives can become so closely connected to our work that it becomes easy to justify that what we do covers who we are. The unfortunate outcome is an anxious soul.

It is not enough to possess innate leadership qualities or finely-honed leadership skills. Spiritual leadership cannot be reduced to formula or procedure. Our understanding and practices of leadership must embrace the truth that ministry leaders are spiritual leaders first rather than organizational managers. Unfortunately, when faced with diminishing time and space, leaders often opt for pastoral efficiency over the long, slow work of personal transformation. Pretty soon, however, our worn-out strategies of 'soldiering on' crumble under the pressures of ministry. Ultimately, leadership techniques become ineffective if we are experiencing a disintegrated life.

Thankfully, more and more leadership voices are now insisting that leadership development prioritize living in a holistic and congruent way, rather than viewing a holistic life as simply an add-on or just another option. Good leaders, however, must not focus only on inner life development at the expense of the outer competencies required of them. Good leaders recognize the need for both.

Ultimately, leadership techniques become ineffective if we are experiencing a disintegrated life.

Earl Creps aptly describes this both/and way of leading: "Reflection on God's activity among us places leaders in the proper posture for listening to God's voice as the source of direction in ministry and waiting for God's Spirit to empower us in the task. Mechanics become important only as they form a response to God's leading."[2] Creps' description could well define essential ministry practice. Yet creating the space to listen and wait feels counterintuitive. Faced with the pressure of productivity, a certain anxiousness remains to move in a different direction away from the long process of listening.

Working Hard for God

Disintegration can also happen when we assume that the mission of God rests on our hard efforts to make it happen. Many sermons on the Great Commission (Matt 28:16-20) tend to reverberate with the words, "Go!" Rightly, our missional-sending God sends us 'on mission.' And off we run. With a sense of calling and a sincere love for people, we launch out to make Jesus known. We work tirelessly for God, asking Him to fill in the holes we leave behind. Over time, our lives and leadership can melt into unending activity, and we become increasingly consumed with techniques that seek to effectively accomplish the mission. We incorrectly believe that our busyness honors God; if we are not doing, we are not being faithful to His call. Our devotional time with Jesus is often hurried and perfunctory, just so we can get going again.

Unknowingly, mission can become the focal point of our life with God. Our hearts fixate on what we are able to accomplish on God's behalf. The need for ongoing connectedness to God gets pushed aside in favor of more tangible outcomes that offer 'greater' kingdom impact.

The redemptive mission of God certainly includes our committed participation and engagement in the world. However, our hyper-activity of doing good works for God too often supersedes the reality of our living in God's kingdom (Matt 6:33). Jesus indeed invites us to partner with Him in the restorative work of the kingdom, but He is not inviting us to a life of constant activity and burnout.

If we are honest, it is easier to *work for God* than it is to *walk with God.* Working hard for God appeals to our need to feel productive (and to our sense of self-worth). Working for God produces more visible and external results. We would rather serve dinner at the Union Gospel Mission or plan an outreach event than enter into a listening pilgrimage with God. We would rather lead a team meeting than confront our patterns of avoidance and impatience. We would rather preach a sermon (because we receive lot of accolades) than relinquish our self-importance. The problem is that it is possible to live on mission without any interaction with Jesus at all.

The problem is that it is possible to live "on mission" without any interaction with Jesus at all.

When we pursue ministry apart from dependence on the Spirit, our leadership can become self-serving, self-important, and unreflective. Instead of building the kingdom of God, some of us find ourselves building our own little kingdoms. Mission and calling must never subvert our first and primary calling to know Christ personally and experience a transformation of our own hearts. We dare not separate the Great Commandment from the Great Commission.

In fact, Jesus linked His present kingdom explicitly and inseparably with our spiritual and character formation. The rule and reign of love of Christ formed in our hearts becomes the infrastructure of God's mission. To be 'on mission' is to cultivate the life of Christ in us that we might embody His presence to the world. Missiologist Christopher Wright explains: "Mission is not ours; mission is God's. It is not so much the case that God has a mission for his church in the world, but that God has a church for his mission in the world. Mission was not made for the church; the church was made for mission—God's mission."[3] We participate in God's mission as co-workers with God (1 Cor 3:9) when our lives reflect the reality of Christ.

Failure to Take Seriously the Importance of the Soul

Another reason disintegration happens in leaders' lives is that we fail to take seriously the importance of the soul. When I found myself grasping for something more meaningful and fundamentally real, I did not have the language of the soul to describe what I was experiencing. Discussions about the soul are typically framed in terms of being 'saved or unsaved,' 'lost or found.' Beyond that, serious thought or conversation about the soul often seems lacking. Perhaps we have inadvertently ignored the need for caring for our inner life, because we don't understand the soul's value and the importance it plays. Yet, in order to experience wholeness, we need a broader, more robust understanding of the soul. Our soul lies in the deepest part of us and integrates all the fundamental aspects of being human. This is the part of you that no one sees—not even you—but it is real. Your soul matters.

The Soul is Paramount

Our souls are not only real, but our soul's well-being or ill-health guides and influences everything that matters the most to us—everything. Dallas Willard, philosopher at the University of Southern California and considered by some the Father of Spiritual Formation, explains the dominance of the soul in his book, *Renovation of the Heart*, "Fundamental aspects of life, art, sleep, sex, ritual, family, parenting, community, health, and meaningful work are all soul functions; they fail and fall apart to the degree that the soul diminishes."[4] Several years ago, I heard Willard speak and he rephrased it like this: "Your heart runs your life. Whether you attend to it or not, it still runs your life."[5] If you ignore your exhausted, anxious soul, your exhausted, anxious soul is still guiding and shaping your life. The "unfinished places of our soul"[6] unpredictably supersedes all our well-intentioned ways of keeping life in check, no matter how gifted, educated, or charismatic we are. This could be why 'successful' leaders unexpectedly fail. For all of their leadership qualities, the disintegrated soul of a leader will hold the upper hand.

For all of their leadership qualities,
the disintegrated soul of a leader
will hold the upper hand.

This is why Jesus spoke so much about the heart and why Proverbs instructs, "Above all else, guard your heart, for everything you do flows from it" (Prov 4:23). "Above all else…" The writer of this Proverb is essentially saying, "This is what is most real about you. Pay attention and give priority to your heart." Out of this deep place comes the stuff of our everyday lives: disappointment, discouragement, joy, anger, resentment, peace, jealousy, contentment, attentiveness, fear … and on it goes. These things come to define and shape our lives. Leadership influence has always been, whether we recognize it or not, an extension of who we are—the real us, for better or for worse.

When we forego an appreciation for the soul, we lose the ability to make sense and attach meaning to our experiences. We focus on tweaking the exterior of our lives, yet we continue to live with hidden shadow realities. Many pastors would nod in agreement with Job: "I have no peace, no quietness; I have no rest but only turmoil" (3:26). As one vulnerable ministry leader recently confessed on social media, "I am so tired of being depressed, confused, and barely making it." Leaders must discover ways of leading that will allow them to structure their lives and ministries around the ongoing health of their souls.

No One Sets out to Neglect Their Soul

In my experience, there remains a surprising discrepancy between a leader's perceived well-being and a leader's actual well-being. Yet, no one actually says to themselves, "I want to intentionally ignore my inner life." Neglect of the soul is more of a benign neglect often brought on by the relentless pace, distractions, and pressures of everyday life and ministry.

Mike pastored a large church and assured everyone he was on top of his world. One Sunday, Mike was preaching on Galatians 6:9, "Be not weary in doing good," as a way to stir his congregation to greater commitment. Suddenly, he stopped short. He began to weep uncontrollably and was unable to collect himself. Later, he confided that when the words, "Be not weary in doing good…" left his mouth, a tsunami flooded his soul. A weariness and disintegration had settled in Mike's soul in a way that had remained unnoticed. Leaders must remain aware that, as with Mike, there comes a time when a fragmented soul, if not acknowledged, will show itself in unexpected and destructive ways.

Caring for Our Souls is not Selfish

I recently taught a master's level class called Spiritual Formation and Development. I stressed the importance of daily spiritual practices necessary for a life of integrated wholeness (the function of the soul). After the class, a twenty-something student came up to me and said, "I really loved what you had to say, but it feels so self-indulgent." I tried to hide my surprise that her perception of self-care somehow makes us self-absorbed. I was also surprised that such an understanding still dominated the ministerial mindset, even with those under thirty. I explained to her that we enter into ministry as broken people, and our calling has not negated our tendency toward self-protection, reactivity, avoidance, or anger. We can be biblically faithful and struggle with compulsive behavior, shame, and resentment. We often bring these unnoticed things to our leadership and unintentionally pass them on to those we lead. As Patricia Brown notes,

> The failure of leaders to deal with their own souls, their inner life, is deeply troubling not only for themselves but also for the persons in the misery they cause. The destructive consequences from leaders who fail to work out of a deep sense of their inner self are staggering. … Leaders have a particular responsibility to know what is going on inside their souls.[7]

Self-care also reminds us that we are profoundly limited. Despite what others may expect of us or even what we expect of ourselves, we are not a fire hose of constant work, ceaseless energy, and endless self-giving. Caring for our soul offers freedom to accept the gift of our human limitations.

Ignoring Our Soul Renders Us Incapable of Caring for the Souls of Others

In times of greatest brokenness, awareness of sin, spiritual longing, and questions, people come to our churches to find rest, wholeness, and healing. Many have come to the end of their rope of self-sufficiency, recognizing their need, and feeling desperate for divine intervention and rescue. They rightly see the church as a place to experience such realities.

No doubt as ministry leaders, we hold a sincere concern and desire to provide help for those we lead. Yet the need for peace, comfort, forgiveness, and deliverance are issues of the soul. To care for the souls of others, we must include this awareness that so much of their needed healing begins in the soul. Without an understanding of the soul, the leader may miss how to be involved in this aspect of God's work. Intellectual prowess proves impotent when hunger for spiritual reality is present.

The Benchmark for Authentic Leadership

Who doesn't love an invitation? To receive an invitation means we are not the ones responsible for putting on the party. We don't set the agenda, gather the needed resources, or carry the responsibility of hosting a 'successful' party. The only request is for us to respond by showing up and engaging in the festivities. In the same way, we are invited into something not of our own making but into the festivities of God's kingdom purposes.

We are invited into something not of our own making but into the festivities of God's kingdom purposes.

So, perhaps the best thing we bring to our leadership is not just the self that is educated and capable, skilled and knowledgeable, experienced and efficient. God is the One building His Church. That is not ours to do. Perhaps it is the leader who comes to define his or her leadership as becoming increasingly responsive to—and involved in the things of—the Father (John 5:19) that becomes the benchmark for authentic leadership.

In chapter 2 we consider Scripture's overarching imperative to listen, as a way of being "all there," to God's initiating activity in our lives.

2

Attentive Leadership

"That God speaks is the basic reality of biblical faith. Listening is an act of personal attentiveness that develops in to answering."[1]

"The assumption of spirituality is that always God is doing something before I know it. So the task is not to get God to do something I think needs to be done, but to become aware of what God is doing so that I can respond to it and participate and take delight in it."[2]

Leading from a Place of Hearing

One day while reading through *Discipleship Journal*, published by the Billy Graham Association, a certain page caught my eye. Oddly enough, it was an advertisement. Probably like you, I tend to gloss over advertisements, but a few simple words centered on the page grabbed my attention: "Deep within you there is a place. It is vast and expansive. It is also hard to find."[3] When I read those words, something leaped in me. How did they know?

I remember thinking, "Whatever they are selling, I want one! No, two!" What they were 'selling' was a master's degree in spiritual formation. Spiritual formation? My experience has a name? There were others just like me? And I could get a degree in it? I read the advertisement's fine print, which simply stated, "For more information, contact Spring Arbor University." Unfamiliar with Spring Arbor University, I immediately checked out their website and learned that they offered a three-year online master's degree. Since my early twenties, I felt that God had set in my heart to pursue a master's degree. I was not, however, interested in a degree to simply to have letters behind my name, but a desired a degree that was congruent with my passion and interest. I had just never found anything that compelling—until then.

I felt God calling me to a new place, a place I had never been before, and I didn't hesitate for a moment. The tricky part came when I had to tell my husband that I wanted to attend a university that we had never heard of, to receive a degree in something I knew nothing about, and, "Oh, and by the way, it is going to cost $25,000. So that fishing boat may to have to wait." In his typical, biggest-supporter fashion, he said with a sly smile: "Go for it! I never liked fishing that much anyways." I contacted the school, registered, and was off on a wild adventure with God leading the way.

I was investing my life in response to God's voice, venturing with God into the unknown, and I didn't want to miss a thing.

When people asked me what I was going to do with my degree, I honestly answered, "I don't know. I love the mystery of not knowing." I understood that if I knew where all this would lead, I would get my hands all over it and mess things up. And, then, if I knew how it ended, I would not need faith. To join God on this new adventure meant surrender on many levels. Yet, the invitation was so compelling that surrendering my plans, my time, finances, and doubts did not feel as though I was giving up something. Rather, it felt as though I was stepping to freedom—even joy—to surrender to something born of God. I was investing my life in response to God's voice, venturing with God into the unknown, and I didn't want to miss a thing. This adventure changed everything—from which I have yet to recover.

In an article titled, "Reasons Why Christian Leaders Fail," psychologist Bill Gaultiere points to a study of 3,500 leaders, among whom only one-third finished well. As Gaultiere notes, "Many drop out (usually due to burnout). Some have a moral or ethical failing. The majority plateau (fade into a slow fail)."[4] Of course, there is always the question of why, which has been addressed at some length already as relates to the inner life of the leader. Gaultiere offers the number one reason for leadership failure: "Lack of a Sovereign mindset: Leaders don't see and trust God at work in all their life situations, even hard or bad things. They're not abandoning outcomes to God."[5]

If we believe that God is self-revealing and personal, we will cultivate ways of staying awake to how He is revealing himself to us in a new way.

"A lack of a sovereign mindset..." Whether we recognize it or not, our theology (the truth we hold about God) determines how we engage with life. What we think about God matters—a lot. For example, because I did not understand that God was actively and creatively engaged in my life, I lived as if it was up to me to make life and ministry work. I remained disconnected from the life of the Spirit in me (Gal 5:4).

As well, if we don't believe God is altogether kind and compassionate, when life gets messy, we will doubt His intentions toward us. If we believe that God is self-revealing and personal, we will cultivate ways of staying awake to how He is revealing himself to us in a new way. Without a sovereign mindset, we are simply left with a godless theology and practice. Most importantly, we don't just believe these perspectives; we respond to them with our lives.

A sovereign mindset assures us that God is actively involved in the ins and outs of our daily lives. His Spirit surprises us by continuing to speak, heal, and reveal God's presence. Living with an awareness of God's movement and sovereignty working in all things allows us to surrender our need to force or manipulate outcomes and live more robustly in the world. A great threat for ministry leaders is to be so distracted or unskilled at paying attention that we live with a pinched image of a life with God. At risk is a hindered conversation with God and a weakened sense of God's abiding presence and movement in our lives. Tragically, we can minister from such a place.

Hearing as Attentive Presence

To live with such awareness of God's activity requires a new kind of thinking and moving. We must begin with the assumption that it is God's nature to speak. Thus, we see the compelling and repeated call of Scripture to "Hear!" We see throughout Scripture that listening composes the central act of the people of God. The fact that God speaks finds its roots, in the beginning of all things: "God said ..." (Gen 1:1). Creation listened to God the Voice, and this set into motion the inaugural pattern of response to the Voice that was heard. Therein lies a Hebraic understanding that God is perceived not by sight but by the hearing of His voice. Christine Valters Paintner and Lucy Wynkoop echo the prominence of speech in ancient Hebrew culture: "Speech, especially the Hebrew Scriptures, is the medium of divine self-disclosure. Therefore, the fundamental stance of the person of faith is to listen."[6] In other words, before our obedience, before our service to God, and even before our worship, above all else, we *listen*.

Listening, first and foremost, precedes and forms the fundamental movements of the Christian life and leadership.

In other words, before our obedience, before our service to God, and even before our worship, above all else, we *listen*.

Shâma'

Understanding God as a Voice who speaks gives meaning to the Hebrew word (שָׁמַע) shâma', translated as "hear," "hears," or "listen." The instruction to hear, *shâma'*, significantly appears 1,158 times in the Old Testament! *Shâma'* is a kind of hearing that encompasses a much wider, deeper meaning than simply hearing audibly with the ear. The force and intent of *shâma'* literally means "Listen!" or "Pay attention!" "Be all there!" *Shâma'* challenges careless or halfhearted listening, preoccupied distraction, or lackadaisical focus toward the God who speaks.

Shâma' also carries a forceful commitment not only to remain fully present to that which is spoken but to the obligation to act on what is heard. God equates listening to Him with keeping His commandments. In fact, in the Old Testament, there is no distinct word for "obey." According to Old Testament usage, to listen and to obey is the singular word of *shâma'*. In other words, we have not properly heard until we have act upon what we heard. When we truly listen, we will act differently.

Dâbâr

God's insistence on attentive hearing comes to light when we reconsider Deuteronomy 6:6, which says, "These commandments that I give you today are to be on your hearts." The word translated here as *commandments* is the Hebrew word, *dâbâr*. *Dâbâr* is most often translated, *word*, and means "to bring into order; to lead, to guide, to rule."[7] This means God's words, or commandments, are not meant to be burdensome obligations but are personal, relational, creative, enlivening, and redemptive!

A wonderful Old Testament example of this interplay between this attentive hearing and life-giving obedience is the boy Samuel (1 Samuel). Scripture records that in the night once Samuel recognized the Lord's voice he responded, 'Speak [*dâbâr*], for your servant is listening [*shâma'*]'" (3:10). In a posture of attentiveness, Samuel demonstrated a proper hearing of God's dynamic and enlivening word and the proper human response of surrender. His response might have meant something like this: "Lord, speak your life-giving word to lead and guide me; the word that brings order to my life and restores me, making me whole in every way (*dâbâr*); I am singularly and devotedly attentive to your Voice that I may wholeheartedly surrender to your purposes (*shâma'*)." Samuel's response to God's voice illustrates the unreserved responsiveness for all who would correctly hear.

Another Old Testament example is that of Solomon, who stood set to assume the kingly leadership from his father, David (1 Kgs 3:7-9). God asks Solomon what he would like to receive from him (v. 5). Solomon, fully aware of the arduous responsibilities that lay before him and his equal inadequacy to fulfill such a huge task (v. 7), answers not by requesting long life or riches or the death of his enemies, but for "a listening heart" (v. 9): "Here's what I want: Give me a God-listening heart so I can lead your people well, discerning the difference between good and evil. For who on their own is capable of leading your glorious people?" (vv. 7-9, MSG). The implication is that proper listening stands as a prerequisite for successful spiritual leadership, which takes priority over security, experience, or control. The "prayer for a listening heart" is not simply to be more clever but to be finely attuned to God's guiding presence; an essential part of leading others well.

The "prayer for a listening heart" is not simply to be more clever but to be finely attuned to God's guiding presence; an essential part of leading others well.

A Deeper Kind of Hearing

Jesus also continually invited people into a new and deeper kind of seeing and hearing. In the Gospels, Jesus repeatedly declared a signature phrase: "If anyone has ears to hear, let him hear" (Matt 11:15; 13:9, 43; Mark 4:9, 23; 7:16; 8:18; Luke 8:8; 14:35). Jesus was not singling out those with hearing issues; something else was at play here.

The Greek word *akouō* translated as the word *hear*, is the equivalent of the Hebrew *shâma'* and evokes the same intentional, active, and focused listening with an intent to put the words heard into action. As Leonard Sweet notes, "The primary gateway to the soul is the ear. By definition, the disciples of faith are first and foremost listeners. The very word disciple means 'the one who listens and learns.'"[8]

Michael Quicke submits,

> Let anyone with ears to hear, listen" is not an empty ritual refrain but an urgent encouragement that listeners need to listen with more than their ears with spiritual apprehension. It calls for holistic listening. Hearers have a responsibility to be willing to live in new ways. It involves an intensity of response that casual notice may miss to its peril.[9]

The New Testament offers two corresponding words, rhema and logos, as synonymous for *dâbâr*. To illustrate, in John 1:1, "In the beginning was the Word, and the Word was with God, and the Word was God." The Word *logos* is translated as "saying, sound, speech, or voice."[10] Thus, with resounding familiarity, the *logos* reverberates: "In the beginning was the Voice, and the Voice was with God, and the Voice was God." Offering a straightforward conclusion, Sweet declares, "Christianity is not about 'Do you believe?' but 'Do you hear?'"[11]

Our obedience is explicitly linked to our ability to listen and willingness to respond to what we hear.

Similarly, our English word *obedience* contains the Latin root word *audire*, which means *listening*. *Audire* is the root word from which we get our words like audio and audience. In this way, our obedience is explicitly linked to our ability to listen and willingness to respond to what we hear. This means our obedience is relational in nature (tied to what we personally hear) and not obligatory efforts tied to impersonal concepts or requirements. (Of such is the stuff of religious living.)

The New Testament word *hypakoúō*, translated as *obey*, actually means to hyper-listen, and by implication, to heed or conform to a command or authority.[12] Every parent knows well when their words are ignored or either intentionally or inadvertently 'not heard.' This word *hypakoúō*, (to hyper-listen) conjures up in my mind the picture of a desperate parent looking at a messy room or ignored instructions, and bending down, looking their child squarely in the eyes, and saying, "Listen to me!" This is not about an ability to hear with the ear. What that parent is saying is, "Pay attention to me, and do what I tell you!" Conversely, when a child does as he or she is instructed, a parent may encourage him or her with the words, "Thank you for being such a good listener!"

Good and proper hearing embraces an equally good and proper response.

Parable of the Sower

All three of the Synoptic Gospel writers include the Parable of the Sower, which suggests that all of them considered it a central and memorable aspect of Jesus's teaching (Matt 13:1-23; Mark 4:1-20; Luke 8:4-15). As Klyne Snodgrass points out, "As often noted, the Parable of the Sower is the key parable, a parable about parables, and the guide to understanding the others. It is a parable about the right hearing of parables. This whole section of Mark is a primer on hearing."[13]

Eight times in fourteen verses Jesus admonishes the 'hearers' to hear, i.e., to understand, to respond, to pay attention to how they hear, and to obey what they hear. New Testament scholar Joel Green observes hearing in its greater context:

> Luke is not interested in 'hearing' in general, but a particular kind of hearing—good hearing, authentic hearing, appropriate hearing, the kind of hearing associated with attentiveness (vv. 8, 18), believing (vv. 12-13), and embracing God's word, steadfastness with respect to God's word, and doing God's word (vv. 15, 12).[14]

In the Parable of the Sower, Jesus explains that the seed is the Word (*logos*) but centers the emphasis and focus on the receptivity of the soil. Eugene Peterson notes that the different kinds of soil stand for different kinds of listeners. The analogy of the soil describes four common conditions of the human heart: the hard heart, the shallow heart, the distracted heart, and the attentive heart. In each case, all four soils receive (lit., "hear") the word. The ability to receive the seed and produce fruit directly relates to the condition of the soil (heart), or the ability to hear (*akouō*) the word. Note the contrast that Snodgrass points out between the attentive heart and a hardened heart: "Hearing requires openness and receptivity—openness to God and a willingness to hear and obey, the opposite of a hard heart. Without openness and the willingness to obey, the hearing required is impossible."[15]

Jesus explains in Mark 4:10 that the purpose of His parables was both to reveal truth to the spiritually responsive and to conceal truth from the spiritually indifferent, impassive, or deaf. In telling parables, Jesus intended to nudge people toward receptive and insightful hearing—those things that are needed to experience the abundant life.

In telling parables, Jesus intended to nudge people toward receptive and insightful hearing—those things that are needed to experience the abundant life.

Inattentive Listening: The Deaf Heart

We have a five-year-old granddaughter named Tessa. I called her house one day to find her sobbing uncontrollably. After she gained some composure, I asked Tessa what was wrong. Her mom (our daughter) told her they needed to go to the store, and asked Tessa to get her shoes on. My daughter stressed that if Tessa would not get her shoes on, she would be left behind. Tessa, unwilling or distracted by other things, failed to get her shoes on in time and was, indeed, left behind with her dad. Between her sobs, she replied, "Mommy told me to get my shoes on. But I didn't listen, and so she left me! And it is all my fault!" Tessa recognized that her failure to listen kept her from an outing with her mom.

All throughout Scripture, God laments the inability or the unwillingness of His people to listen. God's concern is reasonable, for to not be heard in any relationship results in a severing of that relationship to some degree. This reoccurring theme of the stubbornness to hear reflects an equally stubbornness of the heart: "Today, if only you would hear his voice, do not harden your hearts as you did at Meribah, as you did that day at Massah in the wilderness" (Ps 95:7b-8).[16]

Examples of how not listening rendered as a form of disobedience (and the consequences of that disobedience) dominates much of Scripture. When God's people fell into evil ways and practices, God wanted to redeem them from the consequences (ruin and captivity) of their disobedience (not listening). Through prophets, God continually invited them to turn away from the evil of their hardened hearts and come back to Him. But God's people continually refused to listen.[17] Jeremiah 11:8 concludes, "But they did not listen or pay attention; instead, they followed the stubbornness of their evil hearts. So I brought on them all the curses of the covenant I had commanded them to follow but that they did not keep."[18]

Deaf, dull (insensible), foolish (no sense of God), stiff-necked, obstinate, and callous are words Scripture describes as those who do not listen. In Mark 4:9-12, at the end of Jesus's telling of the Parable of the Soil, He tells those gathered, "The secret of the kingdom of God has been given to you." However, that truth is concealed from the spiritually indifferent, impassive, or deaf.

When we fail to listen, we remain without understanding, increasingly incapable of discerning kingdom realities.

When we fail to listen, we remain without understanding and, like my granddaughter, Tessa, we become preoccupied and concern ourselves with lesser things. The consequences for leaders exhibiting such behavior are devastating:

We miss our continued calling.

We miss the cues of grace.

We live self-absorbed and self-deceived.

We are deaf to God compelling us toward compassion, justice, and mercy.

We listen to other voices that speak what our itching ears want to hear.

We fail to perceive with understanding.

For all of our 'doing' in ministry, listening remains fundamental. "Do you think all God wants is sacrifice—empty rituals just for show? He wants you to listen to him!" (1 Sam 15:22, MSG). If it is our job to listen, this must mean we are responding to what God is already saying.

The Initiative of God

God not only speaks; He is also the one who initiates conversation. In the grand narrative of Scripture, God continually invites us into a conversation already taking place. In *The Contemplative Pastor*, Eugene Peterson explains,

> The assumption of spirituality is that always God is doing something before I know it. So, the task is not to get God to do something I think needs to be done, but to become aware of what God is doing so that I can respond to it and participate and take delight in it.[19]

So, our faith journey is not so much that we invite God into our lives as much as that we accept God's invitation into His.

So, our faith journey is not so much that we invite God into our lives as much as that we accept God's invitation into His. Like one who walks in late to a meeting, we simply get to enter into what is already taking place. Christopher Wright explains,

> Mission ... is not primarily a matter of our activity or our initiative. Mission, from the point of view of our human endeavor, means the committed participation of God's

> people in the purposes of God for the redemption of the whole creation. The mission is God's. The marvel is that God invites us to join in.[20]

In other words, mission is not what humans do; it is what God is doing.

Pause for a minute, and think of Abraham, Moses, Noah, David, Gideon, Paul, Mary, and other characters of Scripture. Consider the pattern of God's activity that is repeated over and over in their stories:

- God initiates conversation (up to that point they are usually just like us trying to navigate life as best they can);
- God speaks uniquely and personally and invites each person into plans that were not their own.
- God invites them into a grander story not of their own making, and one they could never imagine.
- Each person then has to surrender something of their pride, fears, limitations, preoccupied happiness, or their cherished image of life, to say "yes" to this mysterious, messy, never-before, God-initiated plan.
- Having surrendered, however, God uses them in ways they never imagined; takes them places they never thought they would go, and in the midst of it all, they become more than they had ever hoped to be.

It seems conceivable—if the story of God repeats itself—the more we give ourselves over to God in our leadership, the more we find ourselves in the middle of God's unfolding drama.

In other words, mission is not
what humans do;
it is what God is doing.

I have seen this same pattern of God's unfolding initiative in my life over and over. When you stop and think about it, perhaps you have too. Hearing God's invitation to enter Spring Arbor University's master's program marked the beginning of my understanding of God's nature to draw me into an ongoing story greater than my own. One of the most beautiful things about the biblical narrative is that it reflects a story about God breaking in. He consistently makes the first move and invites us to respond—not as an obligation, but as an invitation. This invitation persuades us to cultivate a radical openness to God doing something different or new.

He consistently makes the first move
and invites us to respond—not as an obligation,
but as an invitation.

In an article titled, "Bonhoeffer Convinced Me to Abandon My Dream," pastor Chase Replogle writes about his dream to start a church, to build "something great and achieve something impactful for the Kingdom."[21] However, when his dream did not unfold as he had planned, his vision became the grounds for his frustrating demands of others, desperate petitions to God, and crushing self-doubts. Everything was judged by the vision. Everything was evaluated by its success. His work became the obsessive desire to actualize what he had envisioned. Bonhoeffer opened his eyes to a new kind of pastoral vision, that instead of his looking for a far-off place, he could have "a clear vision of what God was doing in the present moment"[22] and among the people he was with. Replogle reflects upon this process: "We are called to a project already underway. True visionary leadership is being first to recognize what God has already formed. I'm just trying to pay attention to God, pay attention to my people, and give voice to what I see."[23] Knowing that God is already at work takes a big load off those of us who feel as though our personal performance is the key to our ministry 'success.'

Perhaps the real vision we bring in leadership is the ability to see what God is doing. Only then we can release our plans and expectations, pay attention to the all the ways God is speaking, and then respond with obedience no matter how wildly unpredictable it seems. It seems that the real work is to cultivate an open posture to all the ways we are invited to respond. In our areas of ministry, we can have confidence that God has already set into motion His purposes unique to our calling and context. There is no need to rely on someone else's ministry model, giftedness, resources, or personality.

You have a role in God's creatively unfolding story, and that is what is most needed. Like the Feeding of the 5,000 (Matt 14:16), God calls us to partner with Him in what He is about to do. However, if we don't hold onto the theological conviction that God is always initiating and inviting us into purposes beyond whatever we could imagine, like the disciples, we will contemplate our resources and decide that we could never pull it off.

It seems that the real work is to cultivate
an open posture to all the ways
we are invited to respond.

Additionally, if we are unconvinced that God's ways are completely original, we will expect God to meet us in the same way as before. We will pour our efforts into trying to recreate what He did or what worked in the past instead of looking for what He is doing right now. God is too creative, too inexhaustible, and too personal to rehash the past. There was only one pillar of fire by night, one burning bush, one Jericho, one lapping of water to define leadership, and one blinding light on the Damascus road. God's ways are always original, and they enliven our hearts more than we can imagine. Thus, it seems that the Christian life and the essence of spiritual leadership, is a continual discovery of Jesus in new and unexpected places.

A Leader's First Responsibility

Moses, too, while leading the Israelites for forty years through the desert on a journey to the Promised Land, experienced the adventure of continual discovery with God. Consistently over those years, the people protested a lack of provision, and God always miraculously intervened. On two separate occasions, they grumbled for water to drink. In both instances, the Lord commanded Moses to bring water out of a rock. They were both miracles for sure. It would be a mistake, however, to assume these were two identical occurrences. The first miracle is recorded in Exodus 17:5-6:

> The Lord answered Moses, 'Go out in front of the people. Take with you some of the elders of Israel and take in your hand the staff with which you struck the Nile, and go. I will stand there before you by the rock at Horeb. Strike the rock, and water will come out of it for the people to drink.' So Moses did this in the sight of the elders of Israel.

The second water-from-the-rock account takes place in Numbers 20:7-12:

> The Lord said to Moses, 'Take the staff, and you and your brother Aaron gather the assembly together. Speak to that rock before their eyes and it will pour out its water. You will bring water out of the rock for the community so they and their livestock can drink.' So Moses took the staff from the Lord's presence, just as he commanded him. He and Aaron gathered the assembly together in front of the rock and Moses said to them, 'Listen, you rebels, must we bring you water out of this rock?' Then Moses raised his arm and struck the rock twice with his staff. Water gushed out, and the community and their livestock drank. But the Lord said to Moses and Aaron, 'Because you did not trust in me enough to honor me as holy in the sight of the Israelites, you will not bring this community into the land I give them.'

Standing before the rock, as on a similar occasion, the Lord commanded Moses once again to take up his staff to bring forth water out of the rock. This was the same staff God commanded Moses to take up (Exod 4:2, 17) and perform miracles before Pharaoh. It was the same staff Moses raised and stretched over the water and parted the Red Sea. This was the same staff, the "staff of God" (v. 20) that had previously and miraculously brought water out of a rock and that had come to represent the presence, provision, and power of God. In this moment, when instructed to bring his staff, Moses might have assumed to know what God was going to do. However, God told Moses to take up his staff and speak to the rock—not strike it with his staff. Moses, however, not only struck the rock, he struck it twice. God pronounces an immediate consequence: Moses would not be permitted into the Promised Land.

After so many years of faithful leadership to a stubborn people, why such harshness? This felt like unfair punishment in a moment of justifiable anger and frustration. If Moses forfeited possession of the long-awaited Promised Land over impatience with whiney people, we are all in trouble. (Who among us have not reacted from a place of frustration and outrage?)

However, I don't think reactionary frustration is the reason. Moses was charged not with impatience or impertinence. He was charged with not listening. The first miracle of water showed Moses in his right role as a leader; listening to God's voice and responding in God's ways. The second exposed Moses's inability or unwillingness to hear God's voice outside of reliable and predictable boundaries. Moses's reliance on God's activity in the past resulted in his inability to respond to a fresh movement of God. Similarly, we often fail by trying to recreate what God did in the past instead of looking for what He is doing right now. When we let what is familiar and comfortable replace what Jesus is actually saying or doing now, we miss the peace, strength, the transformation we need in the present moment. Riding on the momentum of what we have done does not take courage; neither does it give priority to listening.

Listening implies a willingness to make God's will our own. Responding in obedient surrender to what we hear implies trust and honors God's rightful place in our lives. To assume how God may move ignores God's life-giving initiative and creative activity. Thus, as leaders when we don't listen, we dishonor God among those we lead. "Because you did not trust in me enough to honor me as holy in the sight of the Israelites..." (Num 20:12). Failure to listen demonstrates contempt for the one speaking.

Moses's reliance on God's activity in the past
resulted in his inability to respond
to a fresh movement of God.

The Promised Land was uncharted territory, and God knew there were new challenges ahead. He said, "you have never been this way before" (Josh 3:4). In this unknown and unfamiliar place, the people would need a leader who would not cling to past promises of success or past assurances of Presence. That new leader would be Joshua. Instead of trying to recreate the past, the leader Joshua would listen to what God was saying and follow Him no matter how outrageous it seemed (1:3-9). For his first assignment, although we may think he would wish to prove himself as a military leader, and contrary to standard military strategy and even common sense, Joshua led God's people in God's baffling way for an inconceivable victory. A leader's first responsibility is to listen to God and respond to a fresh movement of God.

The underpinnings of our ministry must include a willingness to leave behind any expectations and embrace the mystery of the new work God is inviting us into. It is the leader who listens who takes possession of the Promised Land.

Spiritual leadership begins with the assumption that God consistently breaks into our lives and speaks words that are personal, relational, creative, dynamic, and redemptive. These words actively guide, restore, redeem, and bring order to our lives, drawing

---

A leader's first responsibility is to listen to God
and respond to a fresh movement of God.

---

us to God's gracious activity. We can experience and expect this dynamic, initiating grace in our leadership context as we lead from a place of attentive listening. These words, however, invite our participation. So, what part exactly do we play in God's unfolding purposes and ways? What does God's gracious activity look like in our lives? These are the questions we will answer in chapter 3.

3

Courageous Leadership

"Conversion is less acquiescence to a particular set of faith claims and more participation in the unfolding of a particular story."[1]

Grace: The Dynamic Activity of God

As a part of my master's program at Spring Arbor University, I had the privilege of sitting under the tutelage of Willard for a week. Although hearing from him each day was like drinking from a fresh and flowing stream, what I remember most was his simplified definition of grace: "Grace," he said, "is God's activity in our lives."[2]

Grace. Hmmm. Grace has always felt a bit vague to me. I find grace difficult to recognize when it feels so abstract, even elusive. I know grace lies at the foundation of our faith and makes possible our life with God, but its ambiguity makes grace difficult for me to nail down and notice in my life. What exactly is God's grace? I understand grace as a gift; the unmerited kindness of God, yet I am certain that grace is more than a generalized, momentary blessing.

I realize now that grace is not just a noun—a momentary favor or blessing, but also a verb—a currently functioning reality. As the Holy Spirit influences my soul toward peace, comfort, and strength, and so on, this is a work of grace. When I combined these two understandings of grace, I see grace as God's unmerited and benevolent activity in my life.

I see grace as the grand theme of God's story woven into every action of God. For example, consider Ephesians 3: "For by grace you have been saved, through faith—this is not of yourselves, it is the gift of God" (Eph 2:8). Our salvation is a work of grace as a result of the Holy Spirit's initiative and activity. So, a 'work of grace' is the Holy Spirit's ongoing and creative salvation in our lives.

I see grace as the grand theme of
God's story woven into
every action of God.

Unfortunately, we often hold on to a narrow understanding of salvation. Our modern language and emphasis on salvation often speaks of salvation in the past tense: "Jesus saved me," "Jesus rescued me" "Jesus forgave me." Without an understanding of God's current saving work (grace), the focus of the Christian life can be spent trying to pay back somehow for what Jesus did in the past. Payback squarely puts the responsibility of our salvation on our hard work and ability to prove ourselves faithful. The problem comes when we feel as though our faithful payback should be recognized, or at least appreciated.

I remember a conversation I had with a friend who served in a large church for fifteen years. We chatted over coffee, and she shared her despair over recent difficult circumstances. To be fair, these were not light trials but heavy and wearisome for anyone to bear. She was betrayed by a friend, her husband had a nervous breakdown, and she had recently experienced an unexpected career change.

She paused after a sip of coffee, and then blurted out, "After all I have done for Him! This is what I get?" When the focus of our life with God resides on proving ourselves faithful to what Jesus did (and somehow obligating God to reward us) or behaving rightly (to earn God's favor that He might intervene and make life better), then our faith can simply become like cutting good deals with God.

We may also over-emphasize our salvation with respect to a hoped-for future event. We see God as occupying a distant heaven 'out there,' and we hope to someday to meet him there. We sing songs with the anticipatory language of departure: "Some glad morning when this life is o'er, I'll fly away; To a home on God's celestial shore," and tears well up in our eyes. Yes, heaven is for real; and, yes, entering heaven will be a glorious day! I don't think, however, that our living here should be too much different than living there. Living here with a reality of God's near presence counts just as much as living there.

When salvation is thought of only in terms of a past experience, i.e., a one-time moment of decision, or a future reality (positionally), our salvation gets cut off from life in the present. Left alone to manage life on our own forces our salvation into self-sufficiency and harnessing spiritual principles to try to make life work.

When we fail to take seriously that Jesus is actively present, our salvation leaves most of life untouched.

Neither focusing on a past event, nor waiting for a future reality, proves compelling enough to make a difference in our lives on Monday at work with a snarky boss. When we fail to take seriously that Jesus is actively present, our salvation leaves most of life untouched. So, the question is not, "What would Jesus do?" but, "What is Jesus doing?"

Grace, then, embodies the dynamic work of the Holy Spirit currently at work on our behalf (progressive sanctification). In reality, we are "being saved" every day! The Greek word for *save* (*sozo*) indicates an ongoing, present reality that brings continued healing, rescue, and wholeness. It is important to note that we are not the subject of grace; God is.

Notice the active verbs that describe what God does in our lives (grace): God *releases* us from self-sabotaging anger and shame, *restores* joy amid loss and sadness, *comforts* in our grief, *strengthens* our hearts when we doubt, *calls* us into adventure, *heals* our heartache, *calms* our fears, and more. Again, Willard defines salvation as a right-now reality: Salvation is the daily life we receive from God.[3] This means that every day, our salvation is an ever-present grace (activity of the Holy Spirit) crafting us into the character of Jesus for the sake of the world.

This kind of present salvation (grace) becomes sufficient for all we need today (2 Cor 12:9). The Apostle Paul offers a wonderful description of a God who is personally present and continually transforms us into His likeness:

> Whenever, though, they turn to face God as Moses did, God removes the veil and there they are—face-to-face! *They suddenly recognize that God is a living, personal presence, not a piece of chiseled stone* [emphasis added]. And when God is personally present, a living Spirit, that old, constricting legislation is recognized as obsolete. We're free of it! All of us! Nothing between us and God, our faces shining with the brightness of his face. And so, we are transfigured much like the Messiah, our lives gradually becoming brighter and more beautiful as God

> enters our lives and we become like him (2 Cor 3:16-18, MSG).

Perhaps this is why the Apostle Paul began and ended many of his letters to the churches with the phrase, "Grace and peace to you." His blessing on them was that the dynamic saving activity of God might be continually at work in them.

The Role of Responder

If God plays the part of the initiator of grace in our lives, our part logically must embrace that of an attentive responder. Our response to the invitations of the Spirit toward wholeness will always take on the form of surrender. God initiates grace; our part is to offer ourselves to God in ways that enable that work of grace to take hold of our lives. Surrender allows that to happen. If listening is our most basic stance in our Christian life, then surrender is our most basic response to what we hear.

If listening is our most basic stance in our Christian life, then surrender is our most basic response to what we hear.

Since grace is inherently and insistently relational, our surrender is never to mere constructs of rules and morality. Submission to a system of obligations and prohibitions entirely misses the point of following Christ. The capacity to surrender to God's purposes and ways arises out of a growing friendship with God. We surrender to a person. Our ability to surrender will always be grounded in a personal reality of God's grace (movement and activity in our lives). Apart from relationship, surrender is simply an act of detached obligation. In response to relationship, however, surrender becomes an act of trust and devotion.

Surrender confronts our ambition to control our lives and our leadership, as well as our ambition to demand that things go our way. Not once but six times in the Gospel narratives, Jesus says, "For whoever wants to save their life will lose it, but whoever loses their life for me will save it" (Matt 10:39; 16:25; Mark 8:35; Luke 9:24; 17:33; John 12:25). The pull to be our own savior (and everyone else's) remains strong. We embrace the false assumption that things are better when we are in control. We like it when we invite Jesus into our lives, yet when Jesus invites us into His, we get nervous.

Almost instinctively we draw back from the invitation to 'lose' our lives. Surrender can be especially difficult for us as leaders. We are much more comfortable with words like success, self-fulfillment, and personal achievement. We want to know God's will, not so we can surrender to it, but so we can control it. We say we want to 'grow' in our spiritual life, and then we consider the external things we should pursue in helping us achieve that as a reality. Rarely do we ask ourselves, "How can I surrender more?"

Rarely do we ask ourselves,
"How can I surrender more?"

Still, every day we have opportunity to surrender our inclination to live from a place of self-preservation and self-importance. As we offer forgiveness, ask for forgiveness, submit ourselves to others, release need to be right or hold on to bitterness, to choose to bless and not tear down, we give room to transforming grace (redemptive activity of God) to take hold in our lives—and come to find out, in others' lives as well.

As we continually give ourselves over
(surrender) to the unction of grace in our lives,
we become living sacrifices.

The surrender to of our rights, preferences, and ego becomes our true and proper worship. Worship is our response to God revealing himself to us and the intentional surrender of who we are (Rom 12:1-2) in light of who God is. This means that worship is a daily thing and happens in a thousand different ways. Worship could include lifting our hands in praise, holding our tongue from gossip, or bringing groceries to a neighbor. As we continually give ourselves over (surrender) to the unction of grace in our lives, we become living sacrifices.

A Thousand Surrenders

The goal, it seems, is that we might surrender as Mary did to God's unexpected and confusing grace in her life. Mary hears a remarkable story about what is about to unfold in her life. Like each of us, Mary had dreams and plans for her life treasured deep in her heart. Unexpectedly, however, God shows up and alters the entire course of her life, and the result has nothing to do with the storyline she had intended to write for herself. The sudden arrival of the Holy Spirit in our lives seldom looks how we imagined.

The sudden arrival of the Holy Spirit in our lives
seldom looks how we imagined.

At some point in our faith journey, however, we are going to have to decide who is in control. We like the idea of God being in control as long as He behaves Himself and doesn't touch our

401(k). We trust that God's ways are good, but we like to define what goodness is. That usually means life going the way we want. Some of us don't doubt that God loves us and wants the best for us; we just wonder how disruptive His best will be.

Mary could have approached God's intervention in many different ways: anger, bargaining, disbelief, or denial, but she didn't. She didn't try to get out of it. It is funny how most of my prayers seem to center around asking God to change my circumstances. I want God to conform to my cherished plans for my life. How interesting that we don't see any of this in Mary. Not even a hint. She wasn't sideswiped by an unpredictable God who doesn't stay in His box. This, indeed, is a radical stance toward life in a world preoccupied with control.

Joy happens not when we think we finally have
life under control,
but when we can embrace and delight in the
happenings of God in us.

Amazingly, Mary not only embraced God's perplexing ways, but she delighted in them! She broke out in a song of God's goodness! Joy happens, not when all is well, but when we experience ourselves drawn into the whirlwind of God's creative activity in the world. Joy is our response to the conviction that God is at work birthing something in us that is for others. Replogle concurs: "God is building his church; our gratitude comes from the joy of being in on it."[4] It seems that joy happens not when we think we finally have life under control, but when we can embrace and delight in the happenings of God in us. Here is the remarkable thing: Mary breaks into song before she knew the end of the story. I want to respond in the same way! Too often, though, I cannot see beyond my fears. I just want to tuck in, wait it out, and hope for a better scenario before I sing.

"May it be as you have said," Mary says in Luke 1:38. I think she had said "yes" to God's mysterious ways a thousand times before the angel arrived on the scene that day. Mary had cultivated a habit of saying "yes" over and over to God's small, quiet movements in the mundaneness of everyday living. These daily surrenders came to define and mark her life; so, when the angel appeared that day, she was prepared her to freely say "yes" to this inconceivable moment.

God does not require that we live a heroic faith but a faith that is responsive to all the daily invitations to say "yes" no matter how frightful or insignificant they seem. The Christian life is not about a thousand heroic victories, but about a thousand heroic surrenders in the clutter of our days. John Webster observes, "Listening means obedience. … Obedience to God is the lifelong task of giving my consent to the shape which God has for my life. Obedience is letting God put me in the place where I can be the sort of person who I am made by God to be."[5]

Our goal should not be to create a perfect life (because that's an illusion) or a sure-fire church growth strategy (because that's exhausting), but like Mary, to say "yes" to the life God is bringing and the ministry He is revealing. It will always involve surrender—often giving up what we thought ministry would look like. If we do not live with the understanding of a Greater Story being played out, we will be content to settle for methods and formulas to help us manage whatever is not working. In doing so, we can miss God's kingdom purposes in our lives and ministry.

An Ever-Unfolding Adventure

God's ways are simply not our ways and, in fact, often feel maddening. The whole narrative of Scripture, however, assures us that God's are always redemptive—in our lives and in the ways that He uses us. Perhaps the most radical demand of the Christian faith lies in summoning the courage to say "yes" to the present work of God that interrupts our lives. Being a Christ follower means we live differently. We don't live grasping for anything we think will take away our fears (but never does). We surrender those things and allow God to define our lives.

Allowing God to define our lives requires a steadfast confidence that whatever place in which we find ourselves, we can know God is doing His best work in our lives.

Allowing God to define our lives requires a steadfast confidence that whatever place in which we find ourselves, we can know God is doing His best work in our lives. I wrote this to a friend a few years ago when I was faced with a health crisis:

> There is a grace and peace in all this. Grace and peace are not things I conjured up. They are wonderful gifts from God. I am not so much consumed with expecting a certain outcome as much as I am mindful of all the ways, not just physically, that God wants to heal me. I refuse to get so caught up in the crisis of this moment that I fail to recognize the deeper, richer things He offers. Some people are consumed with how God must act; I am more concerned with all the different ways that He comes to me every day. I have long ago given up the need to ask, "Why?" because I know that oftentimes that will never be answered this side of heaven. And what good would it do? Perhaps it is better to live without reasons and sit with things for a while. I am reminded that I have been

> invited to live into a greater story than my own. I believe that. I have an opportunity to give up how I think life should go, and surrender to what has been given, knowing that in doing so, I find life, real life. I don't know how this ends, but I know that redemption (in all its spaciousness) is always near, and that God is good in His faithful in all his ways.

So much of our faith is played out in daily sensing God's Spirit taking us down a path and abandoning (surrendering) ourselves to it. We don't say "yes" to everything that comes down the pike but "yes" to what God is doing no matter how afraid we are. If fear is the only thing keeping you from saying "yes," then that is not a good enough reason to say "no." To continually say "yes" to a different kingdom that invites us to live beyond our fears will always require more of us than we think we can give, yet God invites us to live creatively and bravely knowing we are participating in something greater than ourselves. We can embrace His purposes in our lives as an ever-unfolding adventure that becomes more defined with each step of surrender and obedience.

Ultimately, this ongoing rhythm of God's initiative of grace and our surrendered response will define the constant and essential movements of the spiritual life.

Ultimately, this ongoing rhythm of God's initiative of grace and our surrendered response will define the constant and essential movements of the spiritual life.

A New Place to Begin

So why does this understanding of grace and salvation matter? As ministry leaders, our role is not to solve people's problems or offer them a quick fix to a pressing need. Pastoral care does not mean running around nervously trying to solve people's dilemmas; eliminate their doubts; or put them on the right track by a good idea, intelligent remark, or practical advice. Ministry must have another beginning point.

Many people come to us and want us to help them fix what is not right. Perhaps our role begins with modeling for our people a way of listening and responding to God's creative intent for their lives for themselves. Peterson summarizes the primacy of attentiveness in the role of leaders: "My job is not to solve people's problems or make them happy, but to help them see the grace operating in their lives."[6]

To live as responders requires that we hold to the theological framework that ensures us that our story fits into God's unfolding, ongoing story of grace.

What if our most essential role as a leader includes leading others to recognize their own stories of grace? Perhaps it is to help them recognize that salvation includes accepting Jesus's invitation to be a transforming presence in their lives today; that salvation is less about a moment in time and more about entering into a life with God that invites them to live as grateful responders to all the ways God is weaving them into His kingdom story.

To live as responders requires that we hold to the theological framework that ensures us that our story fits into God's unfolding, ongoing story of grace.

The Courage to Lead

As leaders, we are supposed to know where to go and what to do. If you're like me, you feel the pressure of clearly communicating vision and strategy to lead effectively into the future. So, we read books and go to conferences, looking for new ideas and any advantage we can find to help us lead well into the future. We keenly feel the weightiness for fresh wisdom and direction, which is compounded by our complex and uncertain times. We are faced with a lot of unanswered questions: Where are we going? How will we get there? What if it doesn't work? Is it worth the risk? What if no one follows me? What if it upsets some people? Yikes. Sometimes we ask ourselves, "Who signed me up for this?"

In a recent Barna survey,[7] ministry leaders were given a list of ten traits: integrity, authenticity, passion for God, competence, courage, discipline, humility, vision, collaboration, and purpose. These leaders were asked to pick one word from this list of what they would most like to improve about their leadership. The area where they said they wanted the most help was courage (27 percent). Rather than "doing the right thing" (integrity); or "being truthful and reliable" (authenticity); or "being good at what you do" (competence); leaders interestingly chose courage—being "willing to take risks." This was an interesting choice. I am unsure that is what I would have picked. The choice for courage makes sense, however, when considered in light of our discussion. For it is from a place of listening, encounter, and revelation that leaders gain the courage to act.

Courage comes from this: "And your ears shall hear (*shâma'*) a word (*dâbâr*) behind you, saying, 'This is the way, walk in it,' when you turn to the right or when you turn to the left" (Isa 30:21, ESV). Without such a revelation, we will simply be left to our cleverness, subject to all kinds of whims, outside influences, insecurities, and doubts. We will model our ministries that leave out ambiguity or mystery. We will forgo waiting on God and listening for Him. We will constantly be driven to make something, anything, happen. We will settle on what expediently 'works.' We will doggedly pursue self-reliance. We will calculate our success based on our resources (or lack thereof) all the while anxiously fearful that somehow ministry is slipping through our fingers.

Admittedly, with the course, pace, and destination of ministry out of our control, this is a frightening way to lead. Yet, the gospel does not move forward without the courage to leave the familiar behind and journey to a new place. Doing so will take inner courage to act on a revelation given by God and take the risks needed along the way, however counterintuitive that may seem.

Listening gives us the courage to say "yes"
before we know where it all leads,
only to discover it is exactly where
God had in mind all along.

Listening gives us the courage to allow God to craft something specific to our calling and context of ministry, participating with the unique work we are given to do. Listening gives us the courage to abandon where we thought our journey would take us and trust that God is unfolding something far greater than we could imagine or bring about on our own. Listening gives us the courage to say "yes" before we know where it all leads, only to discover it is exactly where God had in mind all along. Listening gives us the courage to step into places that require more of us that we think we have to give, and yet before long, we find ourselves living in ways for which we were created.

Come to think of it … courage sounds very much like faith.

Courage, like faith, is a byproduct of listening. Perhaps it was not courage those leaders wanted most but faith. Faith comes not by our schemes and means, but from hearing. The word faith is based on hearing, not seeing: "Faith comes from what is heard" (Rom 10:17, HCSB); the personal, enlivening, acting, creative Word (*rhēma*) of God. Faith is played out in response to having heard the Voice we have come to know so well: "And how can they know who to trust if they haven't heard of the One who can be trusted?" (Rom 10:14). "But not everybody is ready for this, ready to see and hear and act. Isaiah asked what we all ask at one time or another: 'Does anyone care, God? Is anyone listening and believing a word of it?' The point is: *Before you trust, you have to listen* [emphasis added]. But unless Christ's Word is preached, there's nothing to listen to" (Rom 10:16-17, MSG).

Faith and trust are born out of a listening
that awakens us to a sense of God's
presence and purposes.

Faith and trust are born out of a listening that awakens us to a sense of God's presence and purposes. Perhaps this is why without faith it is impossible to please God (Heb 11:6), and why we are called to live by faith. Faith is living with the awareness that God is already sovereignly at work and can break through at any moment, even when we can't see or understand it. Faith trusts that the direction we are headed leads to the place we need to be and that we can put aside our need to construct the process according to our expectations. This allows us to live with abandon to whatever outcome God is crafting. So perhaps what

God wants most from us is to be fully present to His Voice that calls us to an adventure filled with messiness, joy, hardship, and beauty for His kingdom purposes—not only for us to decide to join Him in, but to invite others along.

The unction of noticing the Holy Spirit's movements in our lives and ministry relies heavily on our ability to listen, to pay attention. Leading from a place of listening may prove the hardest thing we do. Not because we are insincere or lazy, but because every day our attention is consumed and diverted elsewhere. We are more distracted than we think. In chapter 4 we will address and this problem and unpack the ramifications for attentive leadership.

4

Giving Attention to Our Inattention

"Attention is the most powerful tool of the human spirit."[1]

"Everyone is distracted. All the time."[2] —Justin Rosenstein, the Facebook engineer who created the "like" button.

This last summer my husband and I, after much anticipation and planning, visited Venice, Italy, the City of Love. Oh my. The breathtaking architecture, the cozy cafes and authentic Italian cuisine, and St. Mark's Basilica all outmatched any expectations we had. People from all over the world crowded the streets in the ninety-degree weather. Water taxis carried locals and tourists alike everywhere in this carless city. We decided ahead of time that our bucket list included a gondola ride on the Grand Canal. (The wait time proved this not to be an original idea.) We boarded a gondola with a gondolier in his red and white striped shirt and started on our timed thirty-minute trip down the canal. Just minutes into our tour something struck me. People, in gondolas all over the Grand Canal in the City of Love, were on their phones! They had a mere thirty minutes to experience an event of a lifetime, yet, rarely did I see anyone looking up from their screens. I was so distracted about their being distracted that I missed enjoying the ride for myself.

Without much pushback, distraction is a word frequently used to best describe this generation. "The Age of Distraction" proliferates recent book titles and is the subject of countless online articles and recent human studies. We are hyperconnected and have a deluge of information pouring over us all the time. The endless opportunities for reacting and engagement conspire to erode our capacity for deep focus and awareness. Like the couples in Venice, we think we're aware of everything going on around us, but not even a glorious gondola ride down the Grand Canal can pull us out of our distraction.

In an unflinching culture of distraction and preoccupation, there remains a strong resistance to creating the space needed to listen. Ministry leaders are not exempt from this overload of distraction.

Continuous Partial Attention

In 1998, Linda Stone, a former Apple and Microsoft executive, coined a term called "continuous partial attention,"[3] to describe the state in which one is rarely "all there." My kids have that. Most of the time I do, too. We are paying attention but only partially, all the time.

While I am writing these words, my cell phone dings that a ministry colleague is hosting a live, online event. He leads discussions I am usually interested in, so I swipe over to listen in. While I am listening, my daughter texts me with a picture of a flower that would look good in my garden. She follows up with an article for me to read. Returning my attention to writing, flicking past Outlook, I notice an email that FedEx just dropped a package at my front door. I want to see what it is. On my way to the front door to retrieve my package, I receive a notice from my WhatsApp group of a friend's response to our ongoing discussion. Then (I am not making this up!), one of my team leaders calls to chat with me about her family's positive diagnosis with the COVID-19 virus.

All this takes place in less than ten minutes! The problem is, I don't think my experience is the exception. I don't think these kinds of disruptions happen only once in a while. They happen *every* day, *all* the time. Living in a perpetual state of interruption continually feeds our frittering attention span. As I write, it is a wonder I can write a coherent and complete sentence at all. The problem perpetuates itself when we get used to this sense of constant 'crisis.' Every interruption seems like the most important thing in the moment. We don't feel as though we can miss a thing. What if that phone call or email is really important?

Living in a perpetual state of interruption
continually feeds our
frittering attention span.

Continuous partial attention. It is our new normal. Yet, the statistics tell us of the near and far-reaching consequences in our ability to pay attention. For example, Gabe Lyons, founder of Q Ideas shares:[4]

- 64% of car accidents are caused by distracted driving.
- The average student can focus on a given task for only 2 minutes.
- The typical Internet user's online screen focus lasts for an average of 40 seconds.
- The average 25 to 34-year-old spends 2.4 hours per day on social media, while the average 8 to 18-year-old child spends 3.75 hours on social media per day.

Kyle Pearce of DIY Genius adds:[5]

- For young people below the age of 21, they check their phone every 8.6 minutes.
- The average smartphone user will tap, swipe, click their smartphone 2,617 times a day That's 18,000 times a week. Heavy users do this about 5,427 times a day.
- In 2015, 3,477 people were killed, and 391,000 people were injured in motor vehicle crashes involving distracted drivers
- The mere presence of one's smartphone reduces available cognitive capacity.

Information Overload

These statistics are staggering for leaders. With the frantic pace and hustle of ministry, whatever space we could eek out is now abducted into screen time. There is even a risk in sharing these statistics, because I understand that no matter how significant the realities they portray, we tend to glaze right over them. I do the same thing. No matter how compelling the material, our brains quickly divert and grab for the next tidbit of information. Even while reading this book, you have probably been conditioned to skim through it.

With little space for reflection to process what information comes across our eyes, we live in an ongoing state of scattered thinking and little transformation.

With so much information poised just a glance away tugging for your attention, you are probably reading as quickly as possible, hoping to read more productively and efficiently. We think just getting through the book will leave the lasting impact that enticed us to pick it up in the first place. Such efficiency rarely does. With little space for reflection to process what information comes across our eyes, we live in an ongoing state of scattered thinking and little transformation.

The term "poverty of attention" was coined by psychologist, economist, and Nobel Laureate, Herbert A. Simon, when he wrote in 1971,

> [I]n an information-rich world, the wealth of information means a dearth of something else: a scarcity of whatever it is that information consumes. What information consumes is rather obvious: it consumes the attention of its recipients. Hence a wealth of information creates a poverty of attention.[6]

With information penetrating our every waking moment, a poverty of attention inhibits even our best attempts to keep life and ministry together. It becomes difficult to assimilate thoughtful reflection for a sermon, to stay present to a conversation, or to craft a discerning response to a complex issue.

Inattentional Blindness

Recent studies of visual perception have demonstrated how startlingly little we see when we are distracted or not paying attention. This phenomenon is known as "inattentional blindness." Intuitively, we think that if something important happens right in front of us, we will see it. However, studies reveal how we can focus so hard on something that we become blind to the unexpected, even when we are staring right at it—like the person right in front of you such as your neighbor or spouse.

In other words, we are far less aware than we think.

In his studies on inattentional blindness, Arien Mack of the New School for Social Research reported, "I came away from our studies convinced that there's no conscious perception without attention."[7] You may want to read that again. We are blind to that which we are not intentionally attentive. In other words, we are far less aware than we think.

Here's the crazy thing: we are unaware that we are unaware that we are unaware.

The Myth of Multitasking

Recent neurological studies[8] confirm that multitasking is a myth. Human brains do not perform two tasks at the same time. Instead, what is called multitasking is actually fast-toggling. The brain handles tasks sequentially, switching attention from one task to the other and back again, extraordinarily fast. In reality, the brain is performing only one task at a time. This gives the illusion that we are doing both tasks together, but for all of its magnificence, the brain can only concentrate efficiently on one thing at a time.

John Medina, author of *Brain Rules*, notes, "We are biologically incapable of processing attention-rich inputs simultaneously."[9] Incapable! Tell that to my kids who insist they are doing their homework, while the TV is turned on, and they are listening to music through their earbuds. The brain not only juggles tasks, but as it juggles, it loses focus and attention. Multitasking trains the brain to pay attention to distracting things. Ironically, the more a person trains his or her brain to pay attention to distractions, the more he or she gets distracted, and the less able that person is to focus for even a brief period.

It appears that multitasking causes an overload of the brain's processing capacity. Daniel Siegel, associate clinical professor of psychiatry at UCLA Medical School in America, instructs "This is because multitasking denies us essential pauses in our mental space. We need this time to develop our inner resources."[10] This explains a lot of things in my life. Here's the catch: multitasking produces a worsening condition of diminishing returns. In other words, the more we do it, the worse we are at it. "Humph," you say. "I am fine. I am not a distracted person!" Here are the synonyms for the word "distracted" from Thesaurus.com: panicked, distressed, frenzied, distraught, and disturbed. How often have you used one of those words this week? Come to find out, you are *not* fine.

This explains a lot of things in my life.

A few months ago, my husband and I were having lunch at a local restaurant when we got a frantic call from our son-in-law, Aric.

"Bria [our sweet, one-year-old granddaughter] just has had a seizure! Can you come pick us up and take us to the hospital?" he pleaded.

"Did you call 911?" I asked.

"Yes! I tried and tried, and they didn't answer!"

Weird, I thought. It is not a good day when 911 doesn't answer their calls.

Aric was standing in his driveway when we pulled up with little Bria, limp in his arms. He jumped in the car, and we raced to the nearest medical office. The doctors examined her and quickly decided to call 911 to transport her to the hospital. We followed behind. By the time we got to the hospital, Bria was alert and talkative. The doctor ran some tests, and we waited in her hospital room for the results.

After some anxious waiting, Bria's tests came back normal and we could finally breathe again. It wasn't until then that Aric looked down and realized he wasn't wearing any shoes! (We hadn't noticed either.) He also realized he had forgotten his phone and wallet at home. (I have never known him to leave his phone behind.) My husband and I drove back to their home to retrieve those items. When we got there, we noticed Aric had left the front door wide open and his keys and wallet on the kitchen counter in plain sight.

In that hyper-stimulated, adrenalin-pumping, distressful moment, Aric's ability to notice and process many tasks simultaneously was significantly incapacitated—so much so that Aric was unable to do a simple task like calling 911. We checked his phone, and when he thought he was calling 911, he had dialed 991 … five times! We were relieved to know that 911 was still on the job!

If people cannot see what is right in front of them, how will they hear and respond to a transcendent God?

Daily we minister from this kind of heightened stimulus, unaware that our ability to make decisions, assess and collate details, and compose coherent thoughts are greatly diminished. Can you imagine how this affects our sermon preparation? We can now begin to understand how our 'panicked, distressed, frenzied, distraught, and disturbed' lives form our ministries. The implications of this crisis of attention are staggering for our ministry context. If people cannot see what is right in front of them, how will they hear and respond to a transcendent God? If love is focused attention, how do we love God, ourselves, or others, when our attention is constantly focused on other things?

Attention Economy

Your attention is big money. Economists call our modern state an "attention economy." Tech companies vigorously strategize how to entice users into spending more and more minutes on their sites because companies can get your money if, and only if, they can get your attention. In other words, your attention is for sale to the highest bidder. Attention is the new economy. Tristan Harris, a former product philosopher at Google (what a job title, right?), now turned vocal critic of the tech industry, calls it an "arms race for people's attention."[11] Nir Eyal, 39, author of *Hooked: How to Build Habit-Forming Products*, notes that none of this is an accident. It is all "just as their designers intended."[12] In other words, do not flatter yourself into thinking that you control what you click on. Your attention has been carefully and expensively calculated.

Your attention has been carefully
and expensively calculated.

This is what we have come to know: Our affection, and ultimately our devotion, is shaped by what we give our deepest attention to. Devotion, by its nature, is focused attention. In fact, tech companies base their economic lives on it. Ex-Google strategist, James Williams, calls the tech industry "the largest, most standardized, and most centralized form of attentional control in human history."[13] This is the stuff of our everyday lives. We are habitually preoccupied; add to this a culture of 'hurry,' and our obsession to do everything more quickly. We simply end up skimming over our lives.

The Cost of Distraction: Disintegration

Through all of this distraction we are becoming increasingly unable to think well and clearly. The word *distraction* comes from the Latin *distractus*, literally meaning "to draw or pull apart."[14] Ever feel that way? Me too. Author O. Alan Noble articulates what, perhaps, we most often feel:

> My mind is scattered and cloudy most of the time. Probably as a result, I often discover that I'm anxious or depressed or worried about something but I can't remember what, let alone why. There's just too much going on. So when these feelings come, the easiest and most efficient thing to do is unlock my phone. And then the dread mostly goes away, for a little while. A shot of dopamine from Twitter keeps the anxiety away.
>
> It's not just the technology that creates this feeling, it's also how ordered and scheduled and deadlined our lives are. We feel like we are constantly missing out on something or failing to do enough. There are always more shows, exercise, dishes, dieting, organizing, reading, and podcasts to catch up on.[15]

I am concerned about how much I resonate with this. It feels like a perfect description of how my leadership days are played out. Even more concerning are the synonyms for distraction: madness, lunacy, insanity, craziness.[16] This is not good.

Attention is our greatest resource because attention leads to awareness. Yet, because we are so busy, so distracted, we forfeit the ability to hear God's voice. We cannot remain fully present to His creative movements in our life and the unfolding of His will. We cannot be reflective and emotionally aware of what is going on in our hearts and how our life is unfolding, and we live with a diminished capacity to cultivate deep and lasting relationships. We live disconnected from our joys, our pain, beauty, and purpose. When we are distracted, we lose our way.

Blogger Joe Kraus summarizes the dire implications of this distraction: "Simply put, at the heart of creativity, insight, imagination, and humaneness is an ability to pay attention to anything—our ideas, our line of thinking, each other. And that is what's most threatened."[17] Distraction is not simply a small annoyance. Somewhere along the way, we lose the very essence of our self. New York columnist, Andrew Sullivan, in an article on his emotional devastation with technology, alarmingly warns,

> But this new epidemic of distraction is our civilization's specific weakness. And its threat is not so much to our minds, even as they shape-shift under the pressure. The threat is to our souls. At this rate, if the noise does not relent, we might even forget we have any.[18]

For those of us who understand the importance of the soul, your alarm bells should be going off.

I am concerned about how much I resonate with this. It feels like a perfect description of how my leadership days are played out.

This is the backdrop and new reality to which leaders are called to minister. Unfortunately, with the pace and weight of ministry, we remain susceptible to this crisis of attention. We verbally lament our culture's frazzled attention span, yet if we are honest, we know we are tangled up as well. Our brains are exhausted from trying to keep up. So, we miss appointments. We mindlessly pray. We don't have words for a struggling soul. With no room to breathe, we struggle to maintain focus and the energy for the rigorous work of staying fully present—to anything.

For those of us who understand the importance of the soul, your alarm bells should be going off.

We must reclaim mental and emotional territory from the stress of hyper-connection, not just for ourselves but for God's pleasure and the good of others.

God Can Only Be Experienced in the Present Moment

Like the couples on their phones in Venice, technology is notorious for yanking us out of the present moment. We've all seen pictures (or experienced it ourselves) of four people gathered around a restaurant table: everyone is looking at their phones, not fully present to those seated with them. We get skilled at false listening. We develop strategies to act like we're listening to reduce the rigorous work of true attention.

As humans, we are 'wired' to live outside of the moment. We live in past regrets or glories and get stuck there, or we are constantly looking ahead waiting for something more promising or more exciting to arrive. Once it arrives, however, it rarely matches our anticipation. Soon we are on to the next 'big thing.' We are not present where we are if we are stuck remembering the past or thinking ahead. What we miss is the experience of our actual life.

In my own experience, I spend much of my time thinking about my next class (that I am teaching), my next meeting (that I am leading), or my next sermon (that I am preaching). I spend the present moment preparing for the future moment. My mind ping-pongs from one thought or one task to another, so I can be on to the coming obligation. Staying present could be one of the hardest things we do. Again, Sullivan succinctly summarizes, "You are where your attention is."[19] Apparently, we are not often where we think we are, and we are always on the move.

Most important to understand is this: God can only be experienced in the present moment. He cannot be experienced in the past or the future. Your soul is only connected to God in real-time: right now. Thus, your ability to notice and respond to God is limited only to the moment you are in now. Mental health counselor and theologian, Jenna Perrine, shares some interesting insights about brain science.[20] She summarizes that we have two distinct and opposite ways of interacting with the world: the Default Network and the Direct Experience Network.

Apparently, we are not often where we think we are, and we are always on the move.

The Narrative Brain Network is active when we are thinking about ourselves, planning, daydreaming, or ruminating. This is the Network we inhabit by default. The Narrative Brain Network engages quickly throughout our day and actively works at solving problems, strategizing, assessing, and dwelling in the past or future. It is useful for self-awareness, future planning, accomplishing goals, considering another person's perspective, moral reasoning, and reflective compassion. The Narrative Brain Network, however, is the network that keeps you up at night because you can't turn your mind off.

The Narrative Brain Network, however, can also become a distraction from the present moment because it allows our mind to wander. Imagine yourself eating your favorite oh-so-moist carrot cake with cream cheese frosting (with walnuts), but you start thinking about yesterday's counseling appointment that didn't go so well, or the dry cleaning you need to pick up on the way home. Before you know it, you look down and the exquisite cake is gone from your plate. You've eaten it without even enjoying a single bite.

Not long ago, I watched the long-awaited online viewing of the award-winning, Broadway musical, "Hamilton: An American Musical." With much anticipation, I sat focused on the rap rendition and musical genius of Lin-Manuel Miranda. Professional dancers in perfect choreography swooped across the screen and performed with spellbinding pitch-perfect voices. Then, however, I thought of the staff dessert get together at our home on Friday, and I wondered what dessert I would serve. Which (with no correlation to dessert) made me think of what to wear to speak on Thursday to the non-profit board of directors on which I serve. Because last time I was definitely underdressed. Rats. Immediately, I was snatched from a perfect moment and anxiously standing in front of an audience. The Narrative Brain Network isn't bad, we just don't want to experience our world exclusively in this way. Living primarily in the Narrative Network can be exhausting.

Contrast that with the Direct Experience Network, where we can be open to the fullness of the present moment typically through our senses. We are 'in the moment,' absorbing information directly. We don't think as much about ourselves, our relationships, or our to do list. In her 2006 memoir, *Eat, Pray, Love*, Elizabeth Gilbert writes about a friend who exclaims, whenever she sees a beautiful place, "It's so beautiful here! I want to come back here someday!"

"It takes all my persuasive powers," writes Gilbert, "to try to convince her that she is already here."[21]

The task is to introduce our brains to quiet,
to perspective, to the fallow spaces
that make listening possible.

Through the Direct Experience Network, we create an internal narrative about our experiences. Take "Hamilton" again. Through this Network, I can remain fully present to and engaged in the powerful two hours of Hamilton.

Attention is closely related to the French word *attendre*, which means "to wait." The Direct Experience Network allows us to expectantly wait long enough to look freshly at what is familiar, to stay available to what unfolds, without judging it as good or bad, and to effortlessly embrace the leisurely pace. The problem is, we haven't been taught how to slow down and switch over to the Direct Experience Network. This is where we listen to God. The task is to introduce our brains to quiet, to perspective, to the fallow spaces that make listening possible.

Listening to God is not just about eliminating distractions. It is about where we put our attention and how our inner life is being ordered. Because the Direct Experience Network is not our default network, it takes practice and training to get our brain to switch there, but the more we do, the easier it becomes.

In an interview with Eugene Peterson, Lucy Shaw asked, "How has being a bestselling author, and scribe for God, affected your soul health? And what is your deepest ambition?"[22] (That's quite a question! I wonder what I would answer.) Peterson poignantly responded, "My deepest ambition, I think, is being present to what is right before me—this piece of creation, this detail of redemption."[23] Regrettably, this definition of ambition has never crossed my mind. How did Peterson, a pastor for over thirty years and prominent public figure learn to stay put in any given moment? It seems that attentive presence may not be impossible after all.

We Must Give Attention to Our Attention

American historical theologian R. Albert Mohler articulates the priority of attentiveness in our spiritual formation: "Our ability to focus attention is not just about the mind, for it is also a reflection of the soul. Our Christian discipleship demands that we give attention to our attention."[24] Attentiveness is less about sincerity or good intentions than it is about paying attention to what we are paying attention to. It requires an intentional and habitual way of living. The good news is, we can partner with the Holy Spirit in the context of spiritual practices to listen and respond to a fresh work of grace. To grow in attentiveness is to grow in wisdom, courage, character, creativity, and capacity for love.

Noting the role that the spiritual disciplines play in all three human dimensions, as Barry Jones explains, "The spiritual disciplines are, at their most basic, means by which we pay attention. They are intentional practices of sustained focus—on God, on His story, on our neighbors and on the condition of our own souls."[25] There is no quick fix to our waning attention span.

However, when intentionally and regularly cultivated, spiritual practices keep us open and available to God when normally our minds would take us elsewhere.

However, when intentionally and regularly
cultivated, spiritual practices keep us open and
available to God when normally
our minds would take us elsewhere.

Neurologist Curt Thompson, in his book, *Anatomy of the Soul*, notes, "All of the spiritual disciplines both require and support the skill of mindful attention, which enables us to set our minds on the Spirit."[26] Spiritual practices involve carving out some kind of space in the clutter and chatter of daily living to call the soul to attentiveness. To this end, the practices for being present must percolate to the top as essential components of leadership. These are the practices to which now we turn our attention.

5

Training in Attentiveness

"Paying attention is the highest form of opening to life and to God."[1]

"To pay attention, is our endless and proper work."[2]

A Cure to Disintegration

Let's return for a minute back to my story. The flurry and pace of ministry left me scattered and separated from God. I knew I had to step into an environment far away from the processes that brought me to this distant place. I knew my disintegrated soul required me to move in a different way. The problem was, I didn't know what a life with God looked like outside of all my striving. I just knew I had to be with Him.

Desperate, the only thing I could think of was to go on a walk. I love the outdoors and moving. Instinctively, I knew I needed to get away from my usual distractions and noise. In an attempt to create a new way of relating to God, I promised myself I wouldn't pray. At least I wouldn't use words. I recognized my penchant to try to manage and manipulate God with my words. I secretly imagined that if I said a prayer loud enough, long enough, said all the right words, then God would … I was done trying to strong-arm God through my scheming prayers. All I wanted now was to receive what He offered apart my intervention or advice. So, I began to walk, day after day, in intentional silence.

Slowly, I began to see things I didn't normally see and hear things I didn't normally hear. I began to have a sense of God's presence. I began to distinguish God's voice from my own and hear words I knew were not my own. (When I tell people God still speaks, they often ask how we hear the voice of God. They rarely want to hear about the long, slow, deep work of listening.)

Incrementally, and in virtually immeasurable ways, I began to cultivate a life with God, a life not lived on the surface of things. I began to let go of the exhausting 'death grip' I had on 'maintaining a vital relationship with God,' in which I was in control. This long, slow work of formation was not about earning brownie points or how I could make life 'work' better, but how I could continually stay attentive and available to God's presence in my life.

In this sacred space, I was more available,
more present, to notice where
God was at work.

Once we realize that God invites us into a relationship, we begin to cultivate different things apart from our achieving. We cultivate practices that keep our hearts focused on and alive to what God is doing. I didn't notice it at first, but the practice of walking created a vital space within me apart from my noise-saturated days. In this sacred space, I was more available, more present, to notice where God was at work. I wouldn't have known to call it such, but my repetitive rhythm of walking composed the essence of the spiritual practices.

Slowly I began to recover my life.

What if I brought these same qualities of attentiveness to my leadership?

What if I began to read Scripture with the same qualities of slowness, reflection, and vulnerability, instead of simply trying to nail down the text for Tuesday's devotional? Perhaps then I would speak more about Scriptures that have captured my heart, stirred up questions, or challenged me personally.

What if I approached prayer not as a technique to manage or manipulate God but as a way of learning to be comfortable in God's presence? Perhaps I might minister from a place of encounter rather than striving.

What if I created a place and space (when I wasn't walking) for silence and being alone with God? Perhaps I might minister from a place of rest and fullness rather than exhaustion and emptiness.

Training in Attentiveness

Craig Barnes in his book, *Extravagant Mercy*, offers a poignant picture of the spiritual practices:

> The Bible often portrays the grace of God as a thin stream of refreshing water that perseveres in a desert land. The only way our parched souls can survive in a spiritually desolate society is to stay close to the stream. That is why we come to worship, read our Bibles, serve others, and pray without ceasing throughout the day. It's all a way of drinking in the grace that keeps us spiritually alive. *The more time we spend by that stream, the more deeply our lives become rooted in God* [emphasis added].[3]

It seems our real task is to stay close to the stream, although this is also not as easy as it sounds. Our scattered lives tend to take us elsewhere. Our technologically driven, hyper-busy, always-plugged-in culture sets us up to function on overdrive. We flit from one thing to another and skim frantically over our lives, hoping something will stick. It rarely does.

How many times have we attended a ministers' conference, read a book, or listened to a podcast, and someone asked, "How was it?"

"Great!" you respond.

"What was your takeaway?"

"There were so many … Umm … where to start … it was just really good all the way around!"

We may have felt inspired or moved, but because we rarely give focused attention for any significant amount of time, what inspired us rarely takes hold in our lives. If we don't intentionally spend time pouring over the material, return to it, digest it, create space to reflect on it, then that book we read or conference we attended will leave little impact, if any, on our lives.

I have certainly been there, done that. Our focus quickly deflects elsewhere, and our frittering leaves us unchanged. Being inspired is not the same as being transformed.

That's where spiritual practices come in.
They keep us attentive long enough
for grace to do its work.

That's where spiritual practices come in. They keep us attentive long enough for grace to do its work. My daily 'liturgy' of walking created the needed space in my life for my heart to attune to a different cue and to allow the Holy Spirit to have free expression in my life. Liturgy refers to small, repeated movements, practices, and phrases that shape us into particular ways of life. Liturgies create new capacities in us over time. Partnering with the Holy Spirit through intentional, focused practices, keep us from frittering our lives away.

Sometimes we associate liturgy exclusively with religious ritual, but liturgy encompasses a much wider range in our lives. We are a liturgical people by nature in the sense that we live by habits, practices, and routines that form to our days. I have a morning liturgy just as you do, and my day feels 'off' if my morning rituals are interrupted. There is a groundedness in repetition. I call these daily habits "rhythms that keep me sane." Repetition, no matter how small, shapes our days. What we do over and over forms our hearts in profound ways.

Repetition, no matter how small,
shapes our days; what we do over and over
forms our hearts in profound ways.

Advertisers understand the power of repetition and its ability to shape our desires. Isn't it odd that Costco always seems to have what I am looking for? The exact color, style, ingredients, quality … it is amazing! How do they do that? Omniscient elves, obviously. Costco relies on advertising's repetitive nature to form our desires. Costco simply gives me what they know I want even when I don't realize what I want … until I see it at Costco. Now I realize my heart (my desire) was unknowingly 'shaped' by advertising's repetitive relentlessness. James K.A. Smith explains,

> It's crucial for us to recognize that our ultimate loves, longings, desires, and cravings are learned. And because love is a habit, our hearts are calibrated through

> imitating exemplars and being immersed in practices that, over time, index our hearts to a certain end. We learn to love, then, not primarily through acquiring knowledge about what we should love but rather through practices that form the habits of *how* we love.[4]

Smith proposes that a devoted heart is learned by repetition. He sums up his thoughts: "Learning to love [God] takes practice.[5]

Spiritual Practices Cultivate a Devoted Heart

The faith tradition in which I was discipled emphasized the 'altar' experience. This meant that after Sunday morning and/or Sunday evening services, there was time allowed for us to come forward to the front of the platform for prayer and to seek God. I met Jesus at such a place. The altar holds a cherished place in many people's hearts, including mine. I encountered God in those moments in ways that marked me forever. The only problem came on Monday. In just a few hours, I was back to my old ways of relating and to my old patterns of behavior. What happened? My devotion was real. My encounter with Jesus was real. Why wasn't I permanently or more thoroughly changed? Lasting devotion, like all our other desires, is shaped by habit-forming liturgies. Spiritual practices pull our hearts toward devotion. Mary Oliver attests, "Attention is the beginning of devotion."[6]

Spiritual practices pull our hearts toward devotion.

Like the rich, young ruler (Mark 10:17-23), no matter how earnest, faithful, or compliant we are, if our hearts have not been trained to love God more than other things, we will choose those things over devotion to God regardless of what we believe.

We have been taught to think we can curate our hearts toward God by gathering more information. Our modern understanding of faith relies heavily on giving mental assent to certain theological constructs and irrefutable facts about Jesus. When I became a Christian at age sixteen, I was instructed to attend a thirteen-week doctrine class for new Christians. After thirteen weeks, if I could give verbiage to the immutable omniscience and omnipotence of God, if I could explain the Trinity or defend the inerrancy of Scripture, I was 'discipled.' Never mind that my anxious heart was still held hostage to fear, greed, envy, and shame. I am not saying doctrine is unimportant! Sound doctrine is essential, but an overly rational view of truth just isn't enough to transform our hearts.

This explains, however, why contemporary Christianity places so much stress on sermons, engaging in Bible studies, reading books, and attending seminars; we assumed that if we just got our facts right, we would live differently. When it comes to living moment-by-moment in the counter-cultural reality of living in the Kingdom, however, our confidence in information is misplaced. Tragically, many Christians go through life trying to love an ideal and be loyal to an abstract principle.

"I just need to get into a Bible study." I hear this a lot. This is how I know someone is soul-weary or struggling in their faith. Their sigh hides a quiet ache that something is missing; something is needed that they can't quite articulate. Their go-to solution? More information: a better Bible study, a better preacher, another podcast, or the latest fad book. Tragically, we have made knowledge and doctrine ends in themselves, leaving a faith barely more effective than mere fact-telling. We have not given a better answer to the realities of our messy lives and the longings of our souls.

In order to grow in our faith, we must begin with an increase in knowledge, there is no argument there; however, growing in faithfulness toward God—being transformed into the image of His Son—depends primarily upon the deepening of the heart's affections for God. Because what we love forms us. Most of what captures our heart and forms our deepest yearnings does not come from didactic teaching but is picked up, snuck into our imagination, or caught like the flu. Again, advertisers know this.

We have not given a better answer to the realities of our messy lives and the longings of our souls.

They don't offer us facts to try to convince us to buy their product; they draw us by appealing to our desire to be thin, handsome, competent, important, rich, envied, and young. They capture our attention with pictures of the 'good life' through our devices.

Jesus understood how our hearts are formed, so He appealed to our desires and imaginations as well. The Gospels are a narrative (story) of Jesus engaging our imaginations by telling stories, asking questions, and showing us a vision of what the kingdom of God looks like. It looks like

- a man helping another out of a ditch;
- a shamed woman being valued and heard;
- a blessing around a campfire;
- fears stilled during a storm;
- provision when there was none;
- searching for one who is lost;

- extravagant generosity;
- calming an anxious heart;
- noticing an outcast;
- restoring a severed relationship … and more.

We read those stories, and our imaginations are stirred that perhaps Jesus could do that for us as well. We imagine a love that knows no barriers and that overcomes sin. We imagine compassion when we can't help ourselves and mercy when we don't deserve it. We imagine being valued and loved just as we are, and we imagine a life different than the one we are living.

We need a new kind of challenge—one that builds not only on a strong biblical foundation but also that shapes our devotion to God in a less didactic and more imaginative way. Most decisively, we need embodied habits that shape our affections, which ultimately transforms us in a way no amount of knowledge can. Spiritual practices help create the habits necessary to shape ongoing faithful devotion to God.

The Neuroscience of Spiritual Practices

No doubt beginning and sustaining any of the spiritual practices from this attentive, repetitive posture is difficult. Most of us are simply not trained in this way. The good news is that our brains are a wonderful companion to our transformation. Our brains were made to learn and change based on our actual lived-out experiences (practices).

Our brains are reforming through intentional practices,
making us more like Jesus.

Neurologically, it is through intentional, focused, and repetitive practices that our brains are rewired for permanent change. In other words, our brains are reforming through intentional practices, making us more like Jesus.

While these practices may feel difficult and awkward at first (like learning to shoot a basketball through a hoop), through focused attention and regular practice, our brains create new neuropath-ways just for them. Eventually, as these practices become habituated in us, our brains begin to choose them as a preferred pathway. In other words, the more we do them, the more we *want* to do them! As Rob Moll explains, "The science of neuroplasticity explains how every experience changes the brain, but it also shows that the most lasting transformation comes by intentional and attentive training."[7] God created our brains amazingly wonderful to connect with Him, as Diane Chandler explains:

> Traditional spiritual practices seem to be rooted in the fact that modern science is only now discovering how brains change. When we give focused attention and regular practice, whether through prayer, study, meditation, journaling or other means of attending to the presence of God, we can experience God in profound ways that lead to permanent changes in our lives.[8]

Jesus provides us with an example of the transformative power of habit when He talked about forgiveness. "But I forgave them!" you protest. So why is there still a sting of pain when you remember the moment of your woundedness? Jesus explained that forgiveness is not just a one-time event. It is not a single grandiose, benevolent moment in time. Forgiveness requires the practice of forgiving, again, and again, and again. In fact, Jesus instructed that forgiveness must be offered 70 X 7 times (Matt

18:22)! No need to do the math. No need to keep track. Jesus offered a symbolism that was related to the task of completing forgiveness. The point is, you keep forgiving until there is no longer any pain attached to the hurtful memory.

Forgiveness is a spiritual discipline, an intentional, repetitive practice that becomes a point of healing every time forgiveness is extended. You just keep on forgiving until one day you wake up, and much to your surprise, you are no longer angry. There is no searing guilt. You are no longer consumed with the need for revenge. The repetitive practice of forgiveness has completed its work. You feel truly free … for the first time.

Khaled Hosseini, in his novel, *The Kite Runner*, beautifully depicts this place of freedom:

> Then I realized something: The last thought had brought no sting with it. Closing Sohrab's door, I wondered if that was how forgiveness budded, not with the fanfare of epiphany, but with pain gathering its things. Packing up and slipping away unannounced in the middle of the night.[9]

Amazingly, when fear and shame no longer control you, you now stand in a place of blessing those who hurt you. You stand at a place of living from a place of wholeness and can offer something life-giving to others.

Forgiveness offers us a glimpse of the power of repetitive practice.

Engaging Our Bodies

My sister loves to climb mountains. Really tall mountains. I think she is crazy. I tell her all the time. As I type, she is climbing the Pyrenees mountains, a range separating Spain and

France. Sue is scaling the sides of these peaks, sleeping in a paper-thin Gortex tent in freezing weather, with most of the supplies she needs for her thirty-day adventure on her back. Oh, and she is alone. Alone. I think she would say that it is part of the adventure. I just shake my head.

One day, I asked her, “Sue, why do you climb mountains?”

Without hesitation, she answered, “Because that is where I feel closest to God."

Me: “Is it because you are so close to death?” I don’t really say that. I just think it.

Although I understand we can experience God anywhere, this seemed like kind of an elaborate scheme to get close to God. The more I thought about it, however, the more I began to see a pattern. As integrated beings, we underestimate the body, mind, and soul connection. There is something about the body-soul connection that we often miss: If we engage our bodies, our souls will follow.

I think this explains the fascination with extreme sports. This is why people jump off the side of a mountain in a squirrel suit, walk a tight rope across an expansive canyon, or go spelunking (climbing through the dark abyss, moist air, and gloomy shapes). Oh my.

There is something about the body-soul
connection that we often miss:
If we engage our bodies,
our souls will follow.

This principle of body-soul connection also included the powerful genius behind Billy Graham’s altar calls. I think Rev.

Graham understood this principle when he invited people to step from their seats and come forward. If he could get people's bodies moving first, their souls would follow. This was my conversion experience. At age sixteen I sat in a small, rural church and listened to a moving message. (I still remember it!) I heard the invitation to come forward to meet Christ, but I didn't leave my pew. I could feel the struggle in my soul: the simple invitation to a life with God and the embarrassment of accepting it publicly. I sat paralyzed. Unexpectedly, the person sitting next to me leaned over and told me they would go forward with me. That was the impetus I needed. As soon as I took my first step, there was such a release and relief in my soul that I burst out crying as I made my way forward.

This is also why I love riding on the back of my husband's motorcycle. When he first told me that he wanted to take up this new hobby, I told him *he* was crazy and refused to go with him. Motorcycles were not a part of my growing up, and I was honestly terrified. The thought of riding exposed with no seatbelts made my hands sweat and my heart race. (Another body-mind connection!) However, once I realized my husband was going to do this with or without me, I didn't want to miss the party. Reluctantly, after my much-insisted practice, I got on. At first, fear made my body so tense I got headaches every time I rode. Gradually, however, I relaxed and settled in.

What I discovered is this: I am most alive when I am most engaged.

Eventually, I found out why people ride motorcycles. The thing about riding motorcycles, like climbing mountains or jumping off skyscrapers is that they engage all of your senses. On the back of a motorcycle, as opposed to a car, I smell the fresh-cut alfalfa, and I feel the cool glacier air on my arms and the baking heat rising from the asphalt at a stoplight. I look into the eyes of the roadkill (yuck!) and intently, and with obsessive regularity, scan the scenery for wandering deer. I hear the distinct and incredibly loud rumble of the Harley Davidson and feel its jerking vibration. All of my senses run fully engaged and on high alert. What I discovered is this: I am most alive when I am most engaged.

This is what spiritual practices do for us—engage our bodies in ways our souls will follow. When we kneel in prayer, raise our hands in worship, prayer walk through a forest or neighborhood, write a prayer of lament, recite the Apostle's Creed, serve hot soup, or remain silent and alone in a world of words and frenzied activity, we engage our souls in profound ways. When we hear, see, smell, and touch, what is common for us, becomes sacred. The embodied spiritual disciplines help us recover and respond to our integrated reality.

Before I finished writing this chapter, I received this email from my sister:

> I have been on the trail twelve days, and most days I have gone into camp very late, which means eating dinner late and getting to bed late after an exhausting trek. Two nights I had horrible weather with rain, thunder, and lightning. I'm so thankful for my hiking umbrella because my raincoat certainly would not keep the rain out at all. My pants got soaked, and I have been shivering. But I have had blessings every day and met wonderful people.

Maybe she is not so crazy after all.

Moving from a Professed Faith to a Practiced Faith

Knowing the transformative power of spiritual practices, none of it matters if the practices are not … well, practiced. For example, knowing about prayer, thinking about prayer, or wanting to pray is not the same as praying. The transformative power of prayer comes not from hanging a Scripture verse about prayer on our wall or underlining a verse in our Bible but from actually praying. We must move from a professed faith to a practiced faith if we are to experience any kind of change. Thinking, talking, and knowing must morph into shared practices and real actions of grace and mercy for the sake of others. Jesus didn't come to give us a belief system.

Rather than accumulate ideas, our faith and our witness to the world must be enacted and embodied to participate in the kingdom Jesus talked so much about.

Rather than accumulate ideas, our faith and our witness to the world must be enacted and embodied to participate in the kingdom Jesus talked so much about.

For example, the invitations of Scripture to trust, call upon, wait, surrender, rest, meditate, gaze, declare, hope, enter, awaken, remember, listen, follow, and the like. If habitually enacted through ongoing, repetitive practices, these enactments are intended to form our hearts and then be lived out in practical ways. For example, when we read, "Whoever dwells in the shelter of the Most High, will rest in the shadow of the Almighty" (Ps 91:1), we love the idea of resting in the shadow of the Most High. To experience this place of rest, however, we must practice, in concrete ways, to dwell. What would a practice of sustained dwelling in God look like?

To keep ourselves from anxiousness will require that we practice remembering God's grace in the past (Ps 116:7). How do we craft remembrance in this week's already-full schedule?

Colossians 3:2 says, "Set your minds on things above." How do we actually focus our ideas, perceptions, and beliefs on God in a world that is so full of distractions?

Ephesians 4:29 says, "Do not let any unwholesome talk come out of your mouths, but only what is helpful for building others up according to their needs, that it may benefit those who listen." To keep ourselves from exaggerating, criticizing, blaming, and gossiping; and to speak only what builds others up, what are the practices that will conform our hearts from hostility to graciousness?

Trappist Monk, Thomas Merton declared, "The spiritual life is first of all a life. It is not merely something to be known or studied. It is to be lived."[10]

Personal Responsiveness

While there are the classic and essential disciplines of Bible reading, prayer, and quiet, alone time with God, spiritual practices can change and adjust according to the current work of grace in our lives. This means the spiritual practices are vast, varied, and embedded in relationship. They allow us to align ourselves with God's present work in our lives.

For example, my office is in my home located at the far end of my house. One day, my daughter came home from school through the garage that leads into our kitchen. Without looking up from my screen, I said (loudly) across the house, "Hi Hon! How did that math test go? Ugg. So sorry. I know how hard you studied. Hey, there are leftovers in the fridge if you are hungry.

They are in the container with the red lid." Immediately I heard the Spirit's voice, "Gail [the Holy Spirit always addresses me kindly by name], you are not all there. You are not fully present." Though I felt a little stunned, I understood the truth of such a revelation. Immediately, I closed my laptop, got up from my chair, and walked into the kitchen. I leaned over the counter from my daughter, looked her directly and steadily into her eyes, and said, "So. Tell me about your test."

That day the Holy Spirit revealed a life-long pattern in me of not being fully present to those around me. My life is full in ways I want it to be full. However, besides my daily responsibilities and commitments, other 'pots' of interest and endeavors always 'boiled on the back burner' of my heart. Each inadvertently stole part of my already limited attention. Consequently, with my distracted heart, I rarely fully gave myself over to the present moment or engaged fully with those with me.

This means the spiritual practices are vast, varied, and embedded in relationship.

This pattern of distraction, of course, pours over into ministry. I find myself holding a different conversation in my head while listening impatiently to someone. I have a hard time writing anything lengthy, like a sermon. So, I write down thoughts on small pieces of paper as they zip through my mind. I often say that I only have a good thought once. If I don't write it down, it is gone forever. It is hard to finish a task, wanting to move on the next thing.

Spiritual practices become life-giving when they are attached not to dead legalism,

but in response to the redemptive
movement of God in our lives.

That day I recognized that the Holy Spirit wanted to bring forth much-needed healing to that part in my life. I knew these deep-seated and detached patterns of relating were not going away because I was now aware of them. So, I decided to partner with the Holy Spirit in this good work. Because I spent so much time in my office on my laptop, I entered into a practice that, when anyone at any time came through my doors, I would immediately close my laptop, walk to the kitchen, looked them in the eyes, and engage them in conversation. What a difference this has made! Every time I respond in this way, a change takes place in my soul. Old ways of disengagement diminish, and those I am with feel valued and loved.

Spiritual practices become life-giving when they are attached not to dead legalism, but in response to the redemptive movement of God in our lives. A powerful function of the spiritual practices is they allow us to keep our hearts in a place of receptivity instead of control. The spiritual disciplines are ways of being, not just what we do. We partner with the Holy Spirit, in the context of spiritual practices, not out of obligation, and with an awareness that we cannot change ourselves. In doing so, we allow the Holy Spirit to do what only He can do to bring about an inner change. To do so always leads to freedom—to become who we were meant to be.

A Season for Everything

Because spiritual practices are a response to God's initiative and movement, we need many tools in our spiritual toolbox to keep us connected to God in different seasons in order to respond to a fresh work of the Spirit refashioning our faith. When seasons change, our tools change. So much of spiritual growth is recognizing new tools in your toolbox. During a deeply sad time, we can write a prayer of lament. Some seasons require worship music, spiritual retreats, or fasting. Other seasons require Christian counseling or a quiet listening pilgrimage. Still other seasons require a new space: the salty air of the ocean, the stillness of the forest, or the beauty of a mountain top. Books were and continue to be some of the most fundamental tools in my spiritual growth, but there was a season when I needed to put the books away. (Painful but necessary.) Hopefully, we are always on a transformation journey with God. Our spiritual life should never be static. Transformation always requires change and a new way of engaging God. This means spiritual practices can look a thousand different ways!

- "Staying" can be a spiritual practice. "Letting go" can be a spiritual practice.
- Listening, before or without speaking, can be a spiritual practice.
- Simplicity, untangling and uncomplicating our lives, can be a spiritual practice.
- Gratitude, speaking honestly, showing kindness, encouraging others can all be spiritual practiced honed-in by repetitive action.

God wants to connect with us, and He created each one of us so uniquely. It makes sense, then, that we would connect with Him in all sorts of unique ways, and that as our lives change, our ways of experiencing faith would change, too. The toolbox makes us feel hopeful. Our journey of faith will prove long and surprising—full of discovery and beauty, silence and singing.

Each in their seasons, full of experiences with God that we can't even yet imagine from where we are right now.

That's what the spiritual disciplines do when authentically pursued. Imperceptibly, spiritual practices engage our souls far beyond what the superficiality of our days ever could; they throw our lives open to the transforming grace and work of God.

Either way, the temptation is to brush these practices off as irrelevant or constricting.

Remember: the spiritual practices are not a means of *works* but a means of *grace* (a work of the Holy Spirit) in response to a fresh movement of God. The spiritual practices simply allow us to set our sails and catch the wind of the Spirit's flow, in ways that are new and good for the world.

It is important to note: if we do not understand that our souls and our ongoing integration are essential to God's kingdom work, we will simply consider spiritual practices as just one more add-on in our already busy lives—and just one more thing to feel guilty about. You may say, "I am fine! Life is good. I don't need this." Or you may say, "I'm not okay, but I am just trying to hold everything together and can't juggle more on my plate." Either way, the temptation is to brush these practices off as irrelevant or constricting. However, if you hold to the theological conviction that God is indeed the one who is actively pursuing His redemptive mission (in which our souls are included), and that our most basic task is to discern His voice and respond unreservedly with our lives, then these practices rise as essential in keeping our hearts open and willing to do so.

We will now look at how and what spiritual practices keep us present to God (chapters 6 and 7); keep us present to ourselves (chapters 8 and 9); and keep us present to others (chapters 10 and11).

6

Present to God

"I ain't gon' die in this pulpit."[1]

"I have no peace, no quietness; I have no rest
but only turmoil" (Job 3:26).

In an article titled, "Soul Care for Servant Leaders," Robert Crosby, president and CEO of Emerge Counseling Ministries, notes that the five essential healthy soul practices for ministry leaders begin first with intimacy with God. No brainer, right? Intimacy with God usually makes it to the top of any spiritual check list.[2] We often use 'intimacy with God' as one of the three-fold missional foci of our churches (intimacy with God; fellowship with others; influence in the world.) We know that intimacy remains essential in our relationship with God, but we are not always sure what that looks like or how that happens.

Pastor Richard Dresselhaus, in an article titled "Three Miles from the Coffee: A Study in Intimacy with God,"[3] explains and laments many ministry leaders' misperceptions, difficulty, and loss of genuine experience of intimacy with God. Looking back over forty years of pastoral ministry, when asked if he had any regrets, Dresselhaus answered, "I would have cultivated a more intimate relationship with God."[4] As a seasoned pastor, his response should emerge as highly significant to all those who come after him. Dresselhaus notes how over time the perpetual obligations and duties of ministry can incrementally and imperceptibly lead ministry leaders away from their original commitment and devotion of Christ. He concludes, "Never allow the pressures of ministry to move us away from the critical mission of our lives—to know God intimately."[5] Yet this priority often gets buried in the urgency and competing demands of the day. We would do well to heed this seasoned pastor's words; to ignore them sets us up to repeat his regrets. Don't wait until you have ministered for forty years to discover that you missed the most important thing.

Don't wait until you have ministered
for forty years to discover that
you missed the most important thing.

As ministry leaders we read or hear:

- "First we must be, before we do."
- "Out of faithful presence flows fruitful ministry."
- "Who we are is more important than what we do. Jesus gets my heart before my hands."
- "Jesus always spends more time getting us ready to lead, than He spends teaching us how to lead. It is a heart thing more than a head thing."

We nod our heads in hearty agreement. "Of course," we say to ourselves (but always appreciate the reminder). The problem comes when we are unsure exactly what intimacy with God looks like or how it happens. Perhaps we have operated on the assumption that because we are ministry leaders, it just happens.

Coming Undone

An understanding of intimacy with God is not as obvious as we may assume. For many years I supposed that intimacy with God was the byproduct of more prayer, deeper Bible study, more effort, or trying harder. If I felt distant from God, I obviously wasn't trying hard enough or devoted enough. I wasn't sure whether I had ever experienced intimacy with God, and I wasn't sure if I could ever reach it. This lack of clarity left me grasping for something that felt elusive and unattainable. Without a clear understanding, I was left to my own efforts and strategies to try to make intimacy happen. All this left me was empty and ragged.

"I ain't gon' die in this pulpit."

In ministry, a misunderstanding of intimacy with God often results in devastating consequences. Recent headlines capture this reoccurring trend:

- "Megachurch Pastor Steps away from Pulpit Because He Feels Far from God, Tired in Soul"[6]

  Why was this pastor stepping away for an extended period of time? He said:

  "I feel so distant from God."

  "I'm tired. And I'm tired in a way that one night of sleep ain't gon' fix. I'm tired in my soul."

  "I want to bring my best self to God."

  "One of the greatest mistakes of pastoring is to think that because you work for God, you're close to God."

  "I ain't gon' die in this pulpit."

This pastor and other leaders demonstrate that it is possible to build a church, an organization, or a team without living in a loving union with Jesus. We can expand a ministry without thinking much of Jesus or relying on Him in the process. Until we can't.

- "Acts 29 CEO Removed Amid Accusations of Abusive Leadership"[7]
- In the wake of sexual misconduct allegations, "Bill Hybels Resigns from Willow Creek"[8]
- "On Easter Megachurch Backs Pastor Indicted for 3.5 Million Fraud"[9]
- "Southern Baptist Leader Frank Page Resigns over 'Morally Inappropriate Relationship'"[10]
- "Former So. Baptist Pastor Darrin Patrick dies of 'self-inflicted gunshot wound' at 49."[11]

Unfortunately, these kinds of headlines occur on a regular basis. I do not mean to demean any of these leaders. There are complex factors, internal and external, and other sides of the story unknown to us. Perhaps when we lack clarity, with little time for reflective thought, we settle for lesser substitutes—things we can see and do that we think will make us successful in the eyes of others. The worst thing we could do is assume it won't happen to us (or that it only happens to megachurch leaders).

Maybe our disintegration doesn't happen in an explosive, public way. We can function relatively well on a daily basis and lead a thriving church, but we live, as Henry David Thoreau describes, "lives of quiet desperation."[12] Secretly, we feel as though our lives are like a house of cards, propped up by an illusion of well-being, that could tumble down at the slightest breath. We are just trying to keep it together.

I've only been pulled over by a policeman once in my life … and it was a doozy. On this particular morning, my oldest daughter, Brittany, was leaving home for the first time for college. I was a mess. I was an even more a mess because it was such a quick and improper goodbye to eighteen years of a now-changing home life. I had to leave the house by 6 a.m. to drive my other daughter, Danae, to the county fair to feed her 4H horse, and we couldn't be late. (There is a bit of horse shaming when your horse is the last to be fed.) Leaving the house, I was sobbing and trying to drive through my tears. Then I saw the flashing red and blue lights. I had never been pulled over before, but I had always promised myself if I ever was, I would not play the "cry" card. And here I was sobbing like a baby. Pulling over, I quickly wiped my tears and tried to gain some composure as the officer approached my car.

"You were going a little fast back there," he said.

"I guess I wasn't aware of that," I honestly answered, trying not to let him hear my shaking voice.

"Is there a reason you were going to fast?" he prodded.

"I am late feeding my daughter's horse at the fair," my voice quivered.

If we are simply trying to hold it together,
there comes a breaking point.

Not letting it go, he pushed again, "Is there a reason you are late getting to the fair?"

And then it happened. I couldn't hold in anymore. It came out like an eruption, "Because I just said goodbye to my daughter, and our family will never be the same again!"

I think I scared him a bit as he took several steps back watching this crazy lady coming undone. The pressures of leadership have a way of relentlessly pushing and prodding us. If we are simply trying to hold it together, there comes a breaking point. We don't always know when, but more than likely, it will probably come out in unraveling ways. As much as we would like to think so, ministry leadership is insufficient for sustainable spiritual vitality in our lives.

I Just Want Out

Distance, soul weariness, exhaustion. As one young pastor notes, ministry without intimacy can leave us saying to ourselves:

> … a certain thought crossed my mind as I was stepping up to preach the first of our four weekend services. It sounded like this: I don't even want to do this. In fact, I don't even like this anymore. Now hear me. I love leading. I love the Church. And I love preaching. That is why this was a red-flag moment for me.
>
> I still don't have the right words to describe that moment and the season around it, but I think you could call it a lot of things. Burnout, fatigue, discouragement and even despondency all seem to have a part in that season's story. I lost my will to fight. I didn't trust the people around me. I was tired and dreaming about my next vacation. I caught myself dreaming about free weekends, living in a community where I was unknown, and the advantages of every other job in the world except the one I was currently filling. I just wanted out.[13]

I have sat with leaders who spoke of being spiritually dry. I hear over and over again how difficult it is in the midst of the busyness and rigors of life and ministry to find or make the time for reading Scripture. It is hard to pray in a disciplined and consistent manner and nearly impossible to set aside time simply to sit and be present to God.

I met with a ministry leader recently who was leaving to serve in a remote area of South America. Knowing the isolation and the mental and physical adjustments that would be needed, I asked her about her personal spiritual practices. How would she stay spiritually grounded in such an unfamiliar environment? She looked at me with a blank stare and awkwardly stammered about reading her Bible.

It is difficult to get the inside
and the outside to come out even.

In another recent conversation, I asked a friend, a highly competent and passionate ministry leader, "What is God inviting you into?" Tears welled up in her eyes. "I want my head and my heart to be congruent. I spend so much time doing. God is leading me in new places, and I am not sure if I am spiritually able to do it," she responded. In the load leadership, it is difficult to get the inside and the outside to come out even.

We cannot offer others what we do not know experientially. Without experiencing spiritual intimacy ourselves, we can only offer theological advice that feels trite and that will rarely hold up under pain and loss. One pastor confided,

> I am really good at preaching and administration. I can cast vision and run a decent board meeting. But when people come to me with their struggles with anger,

> shame, or unforgiveness or in despair, the only thing I can think of to help is to read them a few Bible verses and encourage them to continue to believe God is in control. I tell them to read their Bibles more and assure them I am praying for them. Beyond that, I have little to offer. I am just relieved when they leave.

Surely there must be more we can offer other struggling souls.

The Most Important Thing

Thankfully, Dresselhaus offers a clear understanding of intimacy that we can get our arms around: "The key to intimacy with God is the release of the life of Christ within the heart of the believer."[14] Let me think about that for a moment. This sounds like something God does, not what I do. This means intimacy with God has nothing to do with me harnessing or trying to produce spiritual energy. I cannot make the life of Christ pour into my soul by my best efforts. Intimacy with God is not what I do; intimacy with God is something that happens in me. Our life with God is a derived life; it comes from outside of ourselves.

Intimacy with God is not what I do; intimacy with God is something that happens in me.

Perhaps this idea of "the life of Christ released in you" is what the Apostle Paul captures in the little two-word phrase "in Christ." Paul uses the phrase "in Christ" or "in him" over 160 times in the letters attributed to him. (That's a pretty significant amount!) It seems to be Paul's signature phrase. Once you start looking, you see it everywhere. Some refer to being "in Christ," as "union with Christ," experiencing the ongoing nearness and availability of Christ as an ever-present reality. Nothing is more basic or central to the Christian life than union with Christ. This reality is not reserved for the super-spiritual but describes the normative posture of every Christian.

But I am still left with the question, "How does that happen?"

Several years ago, my kids and I watched the animated movie, "Megamind." With their planet doomed to destruction, the parents of Megamind place the blue, big-headed baby in a spaceship bound for earth. As the spaceship doors are closing, his parents give their final instructions: "And don't forget! The most important thing is …" And the doors close! We sat there with our mouths gaping. We all wanted to know what was the most important thing!

Willard offers the most important 'thing.' In an interview toward the end of his life, Willard was asked to describe in the most concise words how to live the Christian life. (I couldn't wait to find out. I am a just-make-it-simple-for-me person.)

His answer? "Aim at abiding."[15]

No doubt Willard was referring to Jesus's final conversations with His disciples just before His crucifixion where Jesus talked again and again about abiding. Abiding is John's word to describe our union with Christ: "Abide in me, and I in you" (John 15:4, KJV). The Greek word for *abide* means to continue to be present.[16] The task of the Christian life, that of primary importance, Jesus and Willard conclude, is to remain attentively present. No doubt they understood what we have already come to discover: that what we give our deepest attention to forms and shapes our affections and, in the end, our devotion. We love what we pay attention to. Loving God comes, not out of doing, but out of being attentive to and responding to Christ's presence in us. As a result, the life of Christ is released in us and does the work of conforming us into the likeness of Christ.

This is the mystery of becoming like Jesus. One thing is for certain, however: the emphasis is not on us creating intimacy with God but on keeping company with Jesus in such a way that His life flows into ours. (You may wish to take a deep breath and read that again. It is a game changer.) The emphasis in the Christian life moves from trying to achieve spiritual life by doing right things to keeping company with Jesus and allowing His presence to shape us. Keeping company with Jesus isn't a "super-spiritual" idea. Living with an ongoing reality of Jesus's abiding presence is how Jesus described the way all His followers should live. This awareness should be our normal experience and end goal of our faith. When we refer to a relationship with Jesus, this is it.

The emphasis is not on us creating intimacy with God but on keeping company with Jesus in such a way that His life flows into ours.

Can we live this way? Can we sustain keeping company with Jesus in the demands of life and ministry? I contend that it is the most essential thing we do in ministry. It is the gift we offer those we serve. One thing for sure, abiding does not happen naturally or easily in our over-scheduled, frantic lives.

Keeping Company with Jesus

The next logical question we must ask is, "How do we keep company with Jesus in such a way that Jesus becomes an ever-present, shaping influence in our lives?

I love how Jesus describes what "keeping company" with him looks like in Matthew 11:28-30:

> Are you tired? Worn out? Burned out on religion? Come to me. Get away with me and you'll recover your life. I'll show you how to take a real rest. Walk with me and work with me—watch how I do it. Learn the unforced rhythms of grace. I won't lay anything heavy or ill-fitting on you. Keep company with me and you'll learn to live freely and lightly" (Matt 11:28-30, MSG).

Notice Jesus's invitation to those religiously trying to achieve the spiritual life and, yet, chronically anxious they are not doing it well enough: "Come to me." For the weary, Jesus extends an invitation into a deeply held friendship. What does friendship with Jesus look like from these passages? Come close, pay attention, listen carefully. These are the qualities of abiding we are to cultivate to experience intimacy with God. As I stated before, this seems to be our real work in our spiritual life.

"Walk with me and work with me—watch how I do it" (v. 29?). Again, we see Jesus as the one who invites us into what He is already doing. He is already walking, already working, already doing something, and He invites us to join Him in it. Our role, again, is that of a responder. Walking, working, and watching someone carries with it the need to be fully present, to be "all there."

Come close, pay attention, listen carefully. These are the qualities of abiding we are to cultivate to experience intimacy with God.

My husband and I enjoy walks along the Columbia River near our home. Being on a walk with someone is an intimate thing. This experience carries with it the need to pull away from our normal surroundings. The pace is slow and unhurried, keeping in step together (not pushing forward or lagging behind);

undistracted, staying focused and attentive to each other's presence; entering into conversation; and being comfortable with moments of silence.

Working with someone indicates partnering in a shared work. It requires a teachable spirit, a capacity and openness to new ideas, a willingness to put aside (surrender) your own assessment or familiarity to embrace a different way of doing things. Watching someone includes these same qualities of focus, presence, and attentiveness, and curiosity.

In this passage in Matthew 11, Jesus encompasses the wholeness of the spiritual life as a way of being, a responsiveness, and openness to His presence by the indwelling Spirit of God.[17] Intimacy with God, then, isn't a checklist item, but the quality of our every waking minutes. The outcome of all this? Jesus declares some of the most hopeful words I have ever heard: "You'll recover your lives." It sounds too good to be true, but this is why Jesus came (Luke 4:16-19).

Unforced Rhythms of Grace

Jesus further instructs, "Learn the unforced rhythms of grace. I won't lay anything heavy or ill-fitting on you" (Mt 11:29, MSG). An 'unforced rhythm of grace' is a great definition of a spiritual discipline. Learning to walk, watch and work with Jesus takes practice, time, and intentionality—all the ingredients the spiritual practices offer. Spiritual practices create the space and conditions in our hearts for God to do what only He can do—transform us by releasing His life into us. If the release of Christ's life within us empowers the life of intimacy, then the spiritual practices provide the context in which we experience that release.

The effort of the spiritual life comes by cultivating practices that keep our hearts in a place of attentiveness and responsiveness to something God has already begun in our lives. Jesus invites us to radically reorder our lives in such a way that creates an ongoing connectedness/abiding with God, i.e., keep company with Jesus.[18]

Many people misunderstand the nature of spiritual disciplines. They are not "spiritual principles" or "moral guidelines" that we perform to improve our condition. They are not a formula we follow so we can harness divine favor or look godly. We don't practice them to impress God. Rather, the spiritual practices serve a purpose only to the extent that they train our hearts to stay focused, open, willing, attentive, responsive, and submissive (our role!) to the transforming Presence of Christ in us. In turn, we offer others a quality of presence shaped by God.

You Will Live Freely and Lightly

When we come to the end of our own efforts to fix, solve, and make progress in our spiritual lives, we begin to experience the abundant life Jesus offers. Going back to chapter 1 of this book to those leaders who followed me on the nine-month leadership community spiritual formation journey, at the end of the nine months, when I asked them how the spiritual life feels to them now. Almost without exception, they chose the word: freedom. We too can experience this same freedom—freedom from the rigors and demands of religion, and freedom to live wide open to God who offers moment-by-moment grace. Authentic ministry is an overflow of personal abiding.

Authentic ministry is an overflow
of personal abiding.

This process of intimacy with God is for all who follow Jesus. You are first a follower of Jesus, not a ministry leader. The freedom you experience from keeping company with Jesus is for you, inside or outside of leadership. I heard one ministry leader say that he left ministry so he could finally get on with being a Christian. What a tragedy.

So, what are the actual practices that keep us alive and awake to the presence and present work of God in our lives? We are certainly familiar with some: Scripture reading, worship and prayer. If these 'rhythms of grace' feel worn out or have not cultivated a life with Christ for which we had hoped, perhaps we have approached them in the wrong way. My hope is that I might offer you a new way of seeing and hearing that these practices may be new to you. Stay open and curious.

We now look at several of those practices that keep us present to God. Chapter 7 is about reading Scripture devotionally. The chapter considers a way of approaching Scripture not as something we do but as something that is done is us. We are invited to read God's breathing and active Word, in a dynamic way, which includes the idea of being fully present and intently responsive. Chapter 7 also includes a section on prayer. Notably, ministry leaders hold a dismal priority of prayer. We will look at some misunderstandings of prayer and frame prayer as vaster and much more expansive than our typical understanding and practice.

Chapter 8 includes the practices of solitude and Sabbath. One of the most challenging and underused spiritual practices among leaders is the practice of solitude. There is a resistance among leaders. Solitude is counterintuitive to our addiction to productivity. Yet, to lead from a place of attentiveness, creativity, and reflection requires creating space to do so. In a leadership culture of hurry, practicing Sabbath invites us to embrace a different rhythm from the urgency of our days. Our souls, minds, and bodies were never created for unceasing activity or with the ability to bear the unrelenting weight of life and ministry. We will take a look at why intentional rest should top our calendar list as essential.

7

Listening to God in Scripture

"Alive words should be read in an alive manner."
—Author unknown.

"These are not idle words for you—they are your life" (Deuteronomy 32:47).

It can be difficult for ministry leaders to read the Bible for themselves. I know. For years I approached the Bible as a resource to gather an endless amount of information. Viewing my ministry role as a dispenser of information, my goal was to amass as much useful material as possible and nail down the meaning of the text, so I could disperse it. Yet, it is entirely possible to keep acquiring more and more information about the Bible yet be less and less transformed by that knowledge. (Some of the brassiest people I know are the ones with the most biblical knowledge. You probably know them too.)

With so much time spent accumulating this deluge of knowledge, the idea of personal engagement seemed like a luxury or even a nuisance, demanding yet more time and energy I did not want to give. So much of my devotional time felt more like 'doing' time. Sometimes, it felt like doing 'time.' I found myself reading just so I could get through it and check off the box, skimming the Word of God to appease my conscience.

Often when something was not working in my life, I found myself reading the Bible only to find some formula to solve my pressing need of the moment in a just-tell-me-what-to-do kind of way. Over time, my devotions lapsed into an obligatory or cursory endeavor.

It can be difficult for ministry leaders
to read the Bible for themselves.

Quite honestly, the Bible simply became a tool of the job. This was the very thing Jesus accused the Jewish leaders of: "You have your heads in your Bibles constantly because you think you'll find eternal life there. But you miss the forest for the trees. These Scriptures are all about me! And here I am, standing right before you, and you aren't willing to receive from me the life you say you want" (John 5:39-40, MSG). They missed the whole point of Scripture. For them (and for me) the Scriptures had become a book to use, not a means by which we listen and encounter God. Leaders, I challenge you to read the Bible for yourselves—not for your next sermon.

A Different Approach

My underlying assumption of Bible reading was that it was about me so I could become a better Christian. Making Scripture about me caused me to gloss over biblical narratives to search out principles and applicable instructions to serve my own purposes: What takeaway can I use? How can Scripture apply to me and my situation? How can I use Scripture to solve my problem? Of course, a theme running through the New Testament is our becoming mature and "attaining to the whole measure of the fullness of Christ" (Eph 4:13), but to what end, and for what purpose? What if knowing Scripture is not the end in itself?

Once we make Scripture about us, it is fairly easy to get along without it. It becomes just one more thing we can consume. The truth is, I could function pretty well as a leader without a regular intake of Scripture. At least for a while.

In the same way, I noticed that many of my favorite verses were 'promises' addressed to my felt need and how God might help me make life better. For example, a favorite verse for so many people (including me) that stirs up hope is: "For I know the plans I have for you", declares the Lord, "plans to prosper you and not to harm you, plans to give you a future and a hope" (Jer 29:11). We hope in God's blessing and hold on to the assurance that God is crafting a plan for our lives that we yet have to see. Yet, our focus tends to zero in on the prosperous plans that lead us to a desired future (a future which we assume conforms to our definition of prosperity).

The truth is, I could function pretty well as a leader without a regular intake of Scripture.

What if we, instead, assume Scripture is about God and what God is doing? How does that kind of refocus change our approach to Scripture? Looking again at Jeremiah 29, when we refocus our eyes off of our anticipated blessing, we encounter a God who delights in blessing! Read in context of the entire chapter, Jeremiah 29 portrays the grand narrative of God's mission of blessing the people of the world through the nation of Israel's willingness to live faithfully in a conflicting culture. From this perspective, the questions we ask ourselves are: What is this passage saying about God? How is God revealing himself? What is my response? How does this draw me into God's grander story of redemption?

Wright similarly asks, “What would it mean to apply our lives to the Bible instead, assuming the Bible to be the reality—the real story—to which we are called to conform ourselves?”[1] Perhaps this means that God’s Word is most transformative when we understand it is about God and the redemptive story He is telling. Of course, God’s Word is both/and—speaking to and connecting with us personally, revealing God’s character, purposes, and ways. With this new focus, however, we may begin to see Scripture in a new light.

We may now see that the story of David isn’t about five ways we can defeat our giants, but that God helps us discern what is really going on for those whose lives are saturated with the daily certainty and faithfulness of God. (David was the only one there that day who had a grip on reality.)

Perhaps we come to think the story of Peter stepping into the water at Jesus’s invitation not so much about Peter’s lack of faith (for fearfully focusing on the waves that crashed around him), but that the invitations of God always lead us to a place of constant awareness of our constant need of a Savior.

We might view Promised Land not as a place to which the Israelites finally arrived. Instead, their long, arduous journey was all about helping them recognize that the Promised Land—the great promise in God’s redemptive purposes—was a Presence who was continually with them.

Scripture is Meant to Be Read Personally

Without a doubt, sound biblical exposition is foundational to Christianity because we are called to biblical faithfulness. Yet, if our study is just technical in nature, it stops short of Scripture’s intent. Willard, in a class lecture, quipped, "We read Scripture like we are walking through a museum, 'Isn't that nice!'"[2]—leaving us pleasantly moved but not transformed.

I am reminded of God's Word described as living and active, "dividing soul and spirit, joints and marrow, judging the thoughts and attitudes of the heart" (Heb 4:12). This description conjures up a picture surgery being performed on us—more than words on a page, God's alive and operative Word cuts through to the deepest and hidden places of our hearts, exposing our wounded parts, implanting truth, and after it has done its work, brings healing and wholeness. God's Word is something done in us.

God's Word is something done in us.

Someone has said, "Alive words should be read in an alive manner." A synonym for the word *alive* is "dynamic." This means we should read God's breathing and active Word, in a "dynamic" way, which includes the idea of being fully present, thoroughly awake, engaged, eager with anticipation, and intently responsive.

Do you remember the "Magic Eye" that was popular in the 1980s? It required us to look differently, to see through to the 'picture in the picture.' It required us to bring our whole self to the picture with openness, curiosity, and time. It was always exhilarating to discover the mysteriously hidden picture that was not obvious to the unfocused eye.

To approach Scripture in an alive way requires that we bring the same vulnerability, wonder, and humility to the text. Rather than a casual, preoccupied, or hurried approach, this requires that we read Scripture slowly, reflectively, prayerfully, with openness, and curiosity. Often it means doggedly reading and listening to the text over and over.

The temptation is to impose Scripture with certain paradigms we have picked up from our past experiences and learning and impose these ideas into the Scripture passage. Often this keeps us limiting Scripture's truth with our current understanding of that truth. We should assume that our grasp of the truth and the world is very small and needs to grow and expand. We should not be preaching the same sermon in the same way we did twenty years ago but bringing instead a fresh revelation and understanding to our preaching.

We should assume that our grasp of the truth and the world is very small and needs to grow and expand.

When I read Scripture, I typically read a passage at least three times. I realize that the first two times, my heart is still wandering, and I am still in the "check-off the box" mode. Finally, by the third reading, I am settled and focused. I can intentionally switch to my Direct Experience Network (see chapter 4) in which I am present in the moment. This allows me to wait long enough to leisurely look freshly at what is familiar, to stay available to what unfolds and to be fully present to the text. As we spend unhurried time to listen, the text speaks to us and pulls us into actions of thinking, personal self-examination, and ultimately, actionable obedience as we respond to what we hear.

Entering the Story

As modern people, we tend to approach the Bible—particularly its narratives—as events of the past. Our goal, typically, is to extract historical facts and insights, make sense of it, and consider how we might apply it to our lives. The ancient Hebrews had a different view. For them, remembering was an act of reliving. Remembering meant to re-experience it in the present and become participants in the story.

Such was my experience one day in my reading in Mark 10:46-52, the familiar story about blind Bartimaeus. I read the passage and imagined Bartimaeus sitting on a rug. I imagined the noise of the crowd and how frustrating it must have been for Bartimaeus's cries for help to be drowned out. Desperate, unrelenting, and ignoring the rebukes of the crowd, Bartimaeus cries louder. Jesus seems to hear his pleas for mercy, turns, and instructs Bartimaeus to come to Him. Unlike Bartimaeus, I wondered if I wasn't desperate enough in my desire for Jesus to turn to me.

I also noticed that Bartimaeus had to set aside his cloak. Perhaps his cloak was a form of identity or security. I pondered what form of identity or security Jesus would want me to drop to follow him. Yet, sensing there was something more for me there, I wondered, "Lord, what do you want to reveal to my heart?" I read the story slowly again and again, listening to every word. Still, I found myself analyzing the story, when the question Jesus posed to Bartimaeus pierced my heart: "What do you want me to do for you?" I held my breath.

Suddenly, the invitation of Jesus to Bartimaeus was directed at me. I have never had such an invitation. The question cut through my self-defense systems of never asking for too much for fear of being let down. For the first time, I dared to verbalize the desire I kept deep in my heart. Scripture, the living and active

Word of God, knows that is most needed to save us from ourselves (Jas 1:21). Alive words are intended to, like a surgeon's scalpel, cut through our defenses and fears, draw us, and opens up our lives to a grace that saves us.

As ministry leaders, we run the risk of looking at a Scripture passage and saying, "Oh, I know what means. I have preached it a dozen times," and we bring our preconceived judgments to the text. In doing so, we miss how God may be speaking to us in a fresh new way. Some of my most meaningful encounters with God in Scripture were regarding Scriptures with which I was most familiar. Listening is our own act of tenacious openness that we may discover something new.

Listening is our own act of tenacious openness
that we may discover
something new.

The point is to encounter God in the text. In other words, you can know the truth, but if you have not experienced it, it has not set you free. For it is not mere words that redeem our lives, but God himself.

An Encounter with Scripture

As you read the Bible in this way, often you will bump into a passage that causes you to pause. You should pay attention to the pause. In my quiet time one day, I found a written prayer in my devotional based on Scripture I "bumped" into, and it resonated with my soul: "Keep me from self-pity, Lord; and stir me to rise each morning expecting to encounter you and be caught up in your work." Several elements in this prayer caught my eye. I blazed over this beginning phrase, "Keep me from pity," because I was drawn to other parts of the prayer, and because, well, I don't struggle with self-pity. But I felt compelled to go back, read it reflectively, confront my avoidance, and allow its truth to be revealed. It didn't take long for me to recognize the many faces of self-pity that surface in my life disguised as feeling stuck, overlooked, inadequate, unappreciated, anger, resentment … It is not a pretty picture. (Please tell me I am not the only one!) What other words might you use?

The Holy Spirit brought me to a needed place of self-examination through those words. Self-examination is never easy, not simply because we avoid the hard work of making space in our lives to sit long enough for our souls to settle, but because what is real about us is allowed to surface. (I think that's the point!) We would rather skirt around such revelations. None of us want to be confronted with our self-pity or whatever it is that still bubbles beneath the surface of our lives and still pushes us toward disintegration.

To avoid our brokenness, however, keeps us trapped in it. So that morning, I had opportunity to confess my self-pity to the Lord so He could heal my wounded self. That moment offered me a glorious starting point of freedom to leave behind an old pattern of relating to myself and others. I surrendered myself to the work of grace being performed in my soul.

To avoid our brokenness
keeps us trapped in it.

Scripture, the living and active Word of God, knows what most needed to save us from ourselves (Jas 1:21). Like a surgeon's scalpel, alive words cut through our defenses and fears and open up our lives to the grace that saves us. This is where Colossians

3:16, "Let the word of Christ dwell in you richly" becomes a reality in our lives.

Living as Poets

We need to preach Scripture not as an activity detached from our lives; but integral to them, as Matthew 7:24-25 declares:

> These words I speak to you are not incidental additions to your life, homeowner improvements to your standard of living. They are foundational words, words to build a life on. If you work these words into your life, you are like a smart carpenter who built his house on solid rock. Rain poured down, the river flooded, a tornado hit—but nothing moved that house. It was fixed to the rock. (MSG).

Jesus instructed that those who attentively hear (*akouō*) His life-giving, guiding words are to "put into practice" (Matt 7:24, NIV), "act on them" (v. 24, NASB), and "work these words into your life" (v. 24, MSG). These action verbs in these verses are the same Greek word, *poieō*, a highly charged, active word that means to make; to produce, construct, form, fashion; to be the author of; to make a thing out of something; perform; to make something out of nothing.[3]

Even as I write this book, I am aware
that I am crafting an original work
based on what I have 'heard.'

Poieō is where we get the English word *poet*. A poet is a communicator—a person who can imagine and express something in a new, beautiful, and original way. Poets create a work of art out of ordinary things. Jesus was indicating that day that true listening to Scripture allows the Holy Spirit to artistically reveal the truth in us in such a way that unobtrusively compels and draws others to our lives.

Even as I write this book, I am aware that I am crafting an original work based on what I have 'heard.' For many years, I have intently listened to God speak in various ways and written down what I heard. I hope to shape what I have heard into something of beauty that inspires, challenges, and causes us to adjust our gaze long enough to see God and His kingdom with new eyes.

Every time we read God's Word in an alive way and submit to the surgeon's scalpel, we allow the Holy Spirit to artistically craft something beautiful—something original—in us. Then, in our lives and our preaching, our story connects with others on a deep level that allows others to see something they have never seen before, see things in a different light and be inspired to envision a different reality than the one they are living.

For the Sake of the World

Biblical spirituality sticks to the claim that God is actively at work in the unfolding realities of His kingdom through His Word. Reading Scripture, like all spiritual practices, postures us to recognize all the ways God speaks and creatively conforms us to embody the love and character of Christ in the world. This makes our reading of Scripture not just about us, but for the sake of others.

Scripture speaks about living with contentment, putting away anger, extending forgiveness, treating others with kindness and compassion. It calls us to love our spouses, give thanks, rejoice always, and practice gratitude in response to the work of grace in us. Scripture, undergirded by the Holy Spirit, allows us to rightly participate in the mission of God to bless the nations, which includes our family, friends, co-workers, and community.

Listening to God in Prayer

A survey by the Barna Group asked church leaders from a spectrum of denominational backgrounds to list their church's highest priorities. Of the twelve areas of ministry listed, prayer came in dead last. Only 3 percent of pastors identified prayer as a priority. Wow. Dead last. I suppose this should not be too surprising given that prayer has to coexist with a culture of profound busyness and Christian activism. Prayer can seem insignificant or frivolous to the demands of our days or as simply one more thing to do. Prayer may be seen as a bother that slows us down in our let's-get-on-with-it agenda. Other times prayer may feel hollow, boring, or unimaginative.

I have encountered all those aspects of prayer. I understood (and taught) that prayer best expressed itself as conversation, but my prayers always seemed to be a one-sided affair with me asking for things and little time for listening. Jesus repeatedly invites us to ask (Jas 4:2), but usually my prayers hovered simply around petition and pleading. Unfortunately, I only prayed then when I needed something, which often set me up for disappointment when God didn't come through as I thought He should. Often, I only stayed in the place of prayer long enough to make my requests known before rushing out again to resume my busy schedule.

At times, I employed prayer as a technique or formula as a means to manipulate or impress God.

At times, I employed prayer as a technique or formula as a means to manipulate or impress God. I hoped to get God to notice, intervene, and make things better. Too often I got caught up in my ego's attempts to say something profound to God (and to the people around me). Eventually, my experience of prayer crumbled into a place of drudgery and boredom, and little more than a perfunctory act at the beginning of a meeting or hospital bedside. I wished prayer was a 'want to,' but it was more of a 'supposed to.'

I may have been part of the 97 percent who indicated prayer as the lowest priority. After a while it just seemed easier to get on with things at hand that needed to be done. I remember reading 1 Thessalonians 5:17, where Paul instructs, "Pray without ceasing," and thought to myself, "You have got to be kidding! Who has the time (or energy) for that?" Obviously, Paul never had four kids.

Thankfully, prayer is not about pestering God into doing what we want Him to do (because that is exhausting.) Prayer is not about finding the right or eloquent-enough words to say to God. Prayer, as with all of the spiritual practices, helps us respond over and over again to Jesus's invitation to keep company with Him. The focus turns from us praying on our behalf to simply noticing where God is present. Sweet succinctly explains, "Prayer is not getting God to pay attention, but learning to pay attention ourselves to what God is doing."[4]

Prayer, as with all of the spiritual practices,
helps us respond over and over again
to Jesus's invitation to keep
company with Him.

If it is God's nature to speak, as we have come to understand, then prayer becomes not so much about what we say as it is about what we hear. Prayer is first and foremost listening to Jesus, who speaks quietly to us in the depth of our hearts. This means that we must also approach prayer with the same attentive, intentional focus we have learned about lest in our noisy world God's voice gets drowned out.

Prayer takes on a new dimension and purpose from how we have previously experienced it. Rather than a formula or a technique, prayer is an orientation of the soul toward God and His kingdom. It is a stance, a way of being present. Instead of being about a set time and place, or using special words, prayer is a way of listening and turning our hearts toward God, His presence and movements, throughout our day. In his book, *The Pastor in a Secular Age,* Andrew Root notes, "Prayer simply but profoundly directs the pastor's attention back to divine action."[5]

As we refocus our attention, prayer becomes
about getting ourselves to do
what God want us to do and
making God's will our own.

In this way, prayer takes our eyes off of ourselves and is not about us trying to get God to do what we want Him to do. As we refocus our attention on God, prayer becomes about getting ourselves to do what God want us to do and making God's will our own. In the end, prayer is about listening and answering with our lives.

On All Occasions with All Kinds of Prayers

The Apostle Paul gives us a hint of the variedness and richness prayer: "And pray in the Spirit on all occasions with all kinds of prayers and requests" (Eph 6:18). *Pray in the Spirit on all occasions* ... We can turn to God whenever, wherever, and during whatever we are doing or whatever state we are in! Mowing the lawn, changing a diaper, standing in line at the grocery store, or waiting in a doctor's office are all opportunities to pray in the Spirit. We can pray even when we don't feel like it. We don't have to wait for a time when we feel more reverent, grateful, or worthy. I don't know about you, but often I come to the place of prayer and can't even verbalize my thoughts. I am too distressed, too worn out, or too overcome with life. I feel greatly comforted to know that in my weakness, the Spirit intercedes for me in wordless prayer (Rom 8:26).

With all kinds of prayers ... Because prayer is a posture of attentiveness and responsiveness, it is inexhaustibly creative and can take on endless forms. We need not get stuck praying the same prayers in the same way over and over. For example, when I don't have the words to express what is real in my heart, my prayer can even be a sigh. Sometimes that is all I can muster. And it is enough. As Psalm 38:9 reassures us, "My sighing is not hidden from you."

Prayer can be a simple "in the moment" expression that embraces the reality of the present moment or when a moment catches you off guard: When a teary-eyed friend comes to you and asks, "Can we talk?" and under your breath you pray, "Jesus, give me the words." A call from the doctor causes you to breathe, "Lord, I trust you." When you have no words to express your sadness, loss, confusion, or heartbreak: "Lord Jesus, have mercy."

I attended a retreat a few years ago. During a time of communion, when we were served the Lord's Supper, people lined up across the front of the room. We were given instructions to go to someone and have them pray for us. I went forward, and as I held the bread and cup in my hands, I asked the server, "Would be it okay if I don't ask for a prayer request and instead, I just say, 'Thank you?'" I was so overcome with gratitude that my prayer went like this: "Thank you, Jesus. Thank you. Thank you. Thank you. Thank you." These simple words, spoken as a prayer, offered God the most authentic expression of my soul.

These simple words, spoken as a prayer, offered God the most authentic expression to my soul.

From Prayer to Prayerfulness

These kinds of approaches to prayer allow us to move from praying to ongoing prayerfulness. They take us from prayer being a specific time or place, to turning our thoughts and hearts toward God in the ins and outs of our day. This must be what Paul meant when he wrote about praying without ceasing (1 Thess 5:17).[6] Reorienting our understanding of prayer as a way of being attentively present to God requires a willingness to expand our prayers habits and practices of prayer. We must cultivate an openness beyond our familiar experiences of prayer.

The vastness and richness of prayer has been part of the Church's experiences of prayer for centuries. Only now are we beginning to understand and experience the breadth and depth of these prayers again. They have formed the Church from its inception and carried it throughout history. They still have the power to form us today.

Prayer as Liturgy

I was raised in a home with no religious underpinnings whatsoever. The name of Jesus or references to the Bible were never spoken. However, as a little girl, and without any learned knowledge of God, I knew God was real and that I could talk to Him.

Somewhere I had learned the childhood prayer, "Now I lay me down to sleep, I pray the Lord my soul to keep…" I promised myself I would not go to sleep at night until I prayed that prayer. So I did—every night. This simple, liturgical prayer kept me connected to God even before I knew His name. God honored that little prayer and all these years has in miraculous and marvelous ways 'kept my soul.'

This simple, liturgical prayer
kept me connected to God
even before I knew His name.

At age sixteen I accepted Jesus's offer of a life with Him and was discipled in a non-liturgical church tradition. A few years ago, when I began to look more deeply into the practices of liturgical praying, I was surprised how much my soul resonated with these prayers. Up to this point, I had been highly suspicious of what I would have called 'rote prayers;' written prayers that we feared would foster the vain repetitions that Jesus warned about.

However, repetition is crucial for rewiring our brains and forming our hearts. Every day my husband brings me coffee. Does he do it out of duty or because I will be mad if he doesn't? No. He brings me coffee, uncoerced, as an expression of his love. Although he brings me coffee every day, this is not an empty, mindless habit. His coffee ritual reminds us of and sustains our love. When he stops bringing me coffee, we might have a problem. Similarly, the repetitive nature of liturgical prayer focuses our attention on God, which shapes and sustains our love for God.

In reality, many times my praying is on autopilot. Too often my spontaneous prayers have become an empty habit: "Dear Jesus, thank you for..." please help..." My own words are often chronically random and based on what I feel. This sets me up to ignoring important modes of prayer like confession, Scripture prayers, and intercession. I find myself saying words because I need to say something. I am unsure whether I have expressed what is going on in my heart. Every prayer can become rote and empty, even our spontaneous prayers. But it need not be.

A lady recently diagnosed with an early stage of Alzheimer's disease asked to see me. "What can I do for you?" I asked. She looked at me for quite some time. Finding it difficult to put into words what her heart desired, she simply said, "Jesus." I knew what she meant. She wanted something more real long after she couldn't remember how to use her phone or her granddaughter's name. She wanted her soul to commune with God when she no longer had any words. I offered her hope through a simple repeated prayer that, when she has forgotten everything else, these will be the words that will keep her connected to God. The familiarity and repetition of liturgical prayers offers us a way to stop from our striving to find words and allows the truths of our prayers to settle in our souls and form our days.

I offered her hope through a simple repeated prayer that, when she has forgotten everything

else, these will be the words that will
keep her connected to God.

In liturgical prayer, we turn to the words of the Psalms or other portions of Scripture to provide us with words beyond ourselves—words that best express our soul's cry to God. Some of the Scripture prayers I pray on a regular or daily basis include the following:

- I remind myself of God's greatness: "Lord, you are great; You do marvelous things; You alone are God." This is an amalgamation of verses from the Psalms.
- My daily prayer for my children: "Lord, show them your glory" (Ps 90:16).
- To reminded myself of my calling: "The Sovereign LORD has given me an instructed tongue, to know the word that sustains the weary. He wakens me morning by morning, wakens my ear to listen like one being taught" (Isa 50:4).
- I composed a liturgical prayer I pray every morning. Before I get out of bed, I prepare myself for the day: "Lord, before my feet hit the floor, I don't know what today will hold. I trust your ways are good and redemptive in my life. Help me keep in step with you wherever it leads. Be with me, but more importantly, help me be with you."

Liturgical prayers allow us to adopt the prayers of others. As I sit in my brown chair, my morning prayer is borrowed from the book, *Common Prayer*: "Lord, may my soul rise to meet you as the day rises to meet the sun."[7] I love this prayer. I don't know who wrote it, but this prayer reminds me that I cannot make my soul do anything, but every morning I can invite my soul to meet with God. You probably have some verses of your own. Revisit them often. Allow their truths to connect you to God and shape you.

The rich truths others have experienced are offered in addition to our own real, but limited, perspectives. The good news is this is not a situation of liturgy vs. spontaneity. It is both/and, not either/ or. Although any repeated practice can become stale, when practiced with an engaged heart, we feel our prayers fresh and alive as they were intended.

Songs as Prayer

Songs are liturgical in nature. As we sing them over and over and they have the power to shape our thoughts and influence our souls. That's how music has shaped generations of young people. This liturgical power of song explains the pull to return to the songs of our past. They have played such an integral part of our spiritual experiences and formation.

A pastor and friend of my expressed the power of songs as prayer during the most difficult season in his life:

> It's been absolutely brutal, especially emotionally. I was often numb and going through the motions. The one thing that really ministered to me, like never before, was music. I developed a playlist on my phone called "God is With Me." I played those songs over and over and over again; songs like "You Are for Me", "Your Love Defends Me", "I Still Trust You", and oldies like, "He Hideth My Soul" and "Through it All." It's amazing how those songs ministered to me. When I couldn't pray I used those words as my prayer. I walked 30-45 minutes every morning and just listened. The Holy Spirit kept assuring me that through the attacks, through the

> accusations against my character, that it was going to be okay. And he did that primarily through the playlist of the songs I had downloaded.

Praying those songs forged a trust in God's presence, goodness, justice, and safety in a time that threatened his soul.

A Prayer of Surrender

A few weeks ago, a gal requested prayer for herself. She explained her frustration that her life was not going as she planned. She said she prayed and even pleaded with God to help her, but nothing seemed to be happening as she had hoped. While she was speaking, I quietly prayed an in-the-moment prayer: "Lord, give me insight. What's really going on here?" I honestly assured her that God heard her prayers, that He cares, and that He was already at work on her behalf. I shared about Jesus's very real invitation to cast all her cares on Him (1 Pet 5:7).

"I try to let it go, but I keep taking it back," she replied.

Her struggle is the same struggle we, even as leaders, face: the tug between surrender and control. Surrender is rarely easy. It goes against our most basic human intuitions. So, we grab for control. Reality tells us, however, that control is an illusion, and we have less control of things than we realize.

Our penchant for control
is not readily toppled.

I invited this young woman to practice a prayer of surrender. Surrender keeps us in a place of trust. However, because surrender doesn't happen easily, surrender requires that we return to it over and over again. Our penchant for control is not readily toppled. I had her write a prayer of surrender in her own words. It was simplistically beautiful. I encouraged her to pray this prayer often to remind her when she felt anxious and tried to "take back" what she had already offered to Jesus. I hoped this simple prayer would be her guide.

Fixed Times of Prayer

Sometimes when we describe our devotional time, the emphasis tends to be on 'getting filled up for the day.' However, as soon as we leave our devotional 'place,' we often unconsciously 'leave God's presence behind' and get on with our day. It is amazing that we can go through the day without a single thought toward God. The liturgy of fixed times of prayer consists of many intentionally planned, small pauses throughout our day to turn our hearts and thoughts toward God. Fixed times of prayer ensure that we do not get too far into any day without orienting or reorienting ourselves to the presence of God in our lives.

I was driving with my adult daughter the other day when her Apple watch chimed. She looked down and said, "Oh, it is time for me to pause and take a deep breath." Huh? My daughter's new Apple watch came with an automatic reoccurring (liturgical) signal as a reminder for her to stop for a minute and breath. It even set a count down for a minute with an image that connotated breathing in and out. It seems even our hyperdrive culture recognizes the need to embrace a different rhythm in our day, if only momentarily, if we are to live as sane people.

Our experience of prayer becomes vast and expansive and yet another way the life of Christ is poured into our souls.

Once we discover that prayer is turning our attention toward God at any time and in any place, prayer can take on many forms. Our experience of prayer becomes vast and expansive and yet another way to seamlessly keep company with Jesus and the life of Christ is poured into our souls.

An Embodied Act of Ministry

Root notes, "Those who pray, hear God speak."[8] We, then, are to lead others into addressing and being addressed by a speaking God. In turn, we expectantly look for God's redemptive action and ministry in us and those with whom we pray. The practice of prayer, like all the other disciplines, broadens our attention of the world around us. To teach people to pray is to call them into an embodied act of ministry to our neighbors. Peterson concurs: "In our secular age, or perhaps because of it, we must turn our attention to divine action. Prayer is the most concrete way to do so."[9]

Hopefully, in this chapter, you have come to discover a fresh approach to Scripture reading and prayer that brings newness to your ministry. It is this same approach and engaging posture that we bring to chapter 8 as we consider the role of solitude and Sabbath in our lives as we lead others.

8

Listening to God in Solitude

"In the eyes of the world, there is no payoff
sitting on the porch."[1]

"Here's what I want you to do: Find a quiet, secluded place
so you won't be tempted to role-play before God.
Just be there as simply and honestly as you can manage.
The focus will shift from you to God, and you will
begin to sense his grace" (Matt 6:6, MSG).

Clearings

A few months ago, I traveled to the Seattle area with my husband. He was attending a two-day leadership meeting that occurred every several months. I liked to tag along for the opportunity to leave behind my normal obligations at home, work, and busyness. I usually turned those couple of days into a personal retreat. How I looked forward to those much-needed getaways! I usually spent the first part of my retreat going for a walk. I looked forward to a slower pace and no agenda except to listen to God.

The outdoor setting was in a corporate business park that served as headquarters for several national businesses. On this day, while walking I noticed tucked behind the buildings was a small stream that meandered around the tall buildings. How surprising to find placards that told about the animals that lived in or near the stream: otters, muskrats, deer, and a variety of water-loving birds. To the people whizzing by in their cars, this hidden domain went unnoticed. Yet, on a leisurely walk they became a source of delight and amazement.

Soon I came upon a small gravel trail that diverged from the concrete sidewalk. The trail seemed to disappear into a thick grove of trees. The great thing about being unhurried and with no expectation of where your journey will take you is that a small trail looks like an invitation to adventure. Following the trail, I found myself in the middle of a small grove of trees. In the center, someone had built a small wooden platform with nothing on it except a cast iron bench. I sat down on the bench. In that sacred space, I could not see the buildings or hear the rush of cars. Someone, perhaps with a fractured soul, understood the need for a clearing in the midst of the scurry of our days. Mike Yaconelli describes this kind of place:

> I am beginning to understand that life is not [so] much a search for answers, as it is a search for clearings. Clearings are the required stopping places in our lives when our lives get to be too much. A clearing is a place of shelter, peace, rest, safety, quiet, and healing. It is a place where you get your bearings, regroup, inspect the damage, fill out the estimate and make the repairs. It is the place where the mid-course corrections are made. A clearing is a place where you can see what you couldn't see and hear what you couldn't hear.
>
> Clearings are not optional. They are longings in disguise. They are the required rest stops of life when our exhausted souls run out of steam. A clearing is the only place to go when the madness of our lives has left our souls dying, hungering, gasping for oxygen, and nourishment. I am beginning to believe life is not a

> search for jungleless existence, but rather a search for a few clearings in the midst of the jungle.[2]

Instead of escaping the ministry jungle (which is impossible), have you ever thought to look for a clearing? This is where the practice of solitude comes in and why we resist it so much.

Practicing Solitude

Feeling the need to remain on the cutting edge as leaders, we fill every empty space with continual input. We listen to audiobooks while driving. We listen to podcasts while mowing the lawn. We have a book tucked away in our cars just in case a vacant moment opens up. Our mobile devices are always within reach. We are habitually preoccupied. Of course, if we perceive that the weight of our leadership rests on our abilities and intuition, we cannot comprehend any other way of leading.

Feeling the need to remain on the cutting edge as leaders, we fill every empty space with continual input.

To add to this resistance, stopping and unplugging from constant stimulation and our addiction to noise, words, and activity makes us feel anxious. So, we mindlessly turn the radio on when we get into our cars. We might not even be able to imagine what it would be like to be still long enough and quiet enough without an agenda, prayer list, or Bible study plan.

I have worked with ministry leaders long enough to know that for us, a seemingly nonproductive 'activity' as sitting alone in silence can feel like wasted time. We are addicted to productivity. We may complain about being too busy, but a part of us is drawn to a hurried life and the sense of identity we get from being overloaded. We often succumb to the illusion that the busier we are, the more important we are.

The purpose of solitude is not to accomplish anything; and that's what makes us so uncomfortable. Many leaders feel spiritual practices, like solitude, are simply an 'add-on' that they can't afford with already busy schedule. The tasks at hand appear more compelling than sitting and doing nothing. Little in our culture applauds us for stopping or quieting. They don't give out awards for such things. Barbara Brown Taylor quips "In the eyes of the world, there is no payoff sitting on the porch."[3]

Of course, we are always looking for a payoff.

The purpose of solitude is not to accomplish anything; and that's what makes us so uncomfortable.

Scripture tells us God restores our soul by "still waters" (Ps. 23). It does not say by rushing rivers. Where else do we experience God's presence and hear His voice? How do we lead others well without space for reflection? Where else do we go to find the peace, grace, and rest that we need? How do we minister without these things?

Solitude Shapes our Devotion

The purpose of solitude, like all the other spiritual practices, is not to fill our schedules with one more thing to do or feel guilty about not doing. Practicing solitude helps us intentionally shove aside the distractions and obsessions of our days to focus our attention on God that shapes our devotion to God.

In solitude, we push the needed pause button of our lives. To lead from a place of listening, solitude helps us cultivate a listening heart. Like the prophet, Elijah, God often seems to speak in whispers, which may require us to lean in closely, attentively, and in quiet surroundings. Solitude, however, is not a sleepy settling in and is anything but passive. Solitude fosters increased alertness. Quiet and alone, we make room to hear thoughts that come from God and remain open to recognizing his creative movement in our lives once again.

In solitude, the Holy Spirit reveals blind spots we don't know we have because, well, they are blind spots. Stillness becomes a place of encounter. In stillness, we experience the peace and rest where inner chaos begins to settle. It is the refuge we long for. We quietly surrender our need to be in control. We are freed from the burden of being important and capable.

In stillness, we experience the peace and rest where inner chaos begins to settle.

I have a big, brown, overstuffed chair in my office where I meet with God most mornings. A small wooden table sits next to my chair, set with some of my favorite things: books, a candle, a plant, and a frame. The frame, a handmade gift from a friend, contains Scrabble tiles which spell out, "Here I am." This simple phrase offers a place for me to begin in God's presence.[4]

Be Still My Soul

My mind is most often scattered. Sometimes I just can't think. My soul is weary from all of the output required of me. Many responsibilities and obligations suck me dry. The drive to succeed over-powers my best of intentions to live more reflectively. I find myself missing important tasks (like appointments) because I am so distracted.

My brain tells me (usually at about 3:00 PM) that it needs a rest, but there is no time for rest in the middle of the day, so I make a pot of coffee. I am not able to sift through the day's input, discern what is most needed, and figure out what I can let go of. I need a different place and pace where my life can stay put for a moment. Blogger Nick Ross explains,

> When the soul of a person ('that which is essential') is left behind, when we forego a language and appreciation for the soul—when we no longer know or are able to stop long enough to let our souls 'catch up'—the consequences are devastating. The soul of a person, as every poet knows, needs to speak, to muse, to consider and reflect if it is to be well, if it is to act as it should, as a guide for what is most important in our lives. It's not a matter of indulgence. It's a matter of sanity.[5]

The drive to succeed overpowers my best of intentions to live more reflectively.

The Birthplace of Creativity

The space we create when we stop and listen also serves as the birthplace of creativity. The mind is most creative when it is resting. That's why we have such great thoughts and get our best ideas when we are showering, mowing the lawn, or working out. Repetitive things that do not take much thought allow our minds to slip into autopilot. My best thoughts come from that place of disengagement. I always keep a pen and paper nearby. Some mornings, ideas flow faster than I can write them down.

Someone has said, "The whole point of listening is that you are given things you would never come up with on your own."

A survey among 100 top executives asked what contributed most to their ability to lead. Their answer? The space to be creative. Reflect. Be inquisitive. Dream. Listen. Solitude creates an open space where we can leisurely process information and make surprising connections. In this reflective space, our thoughts have a place to settle. Alone time fosters original thinking and allows God-inspired ideas to surface.

One of the best things we bring to our leadership are 'God ideas'. Things we would have never thought of in the push and shove of our days. Pastor Mark Batterson points out, "I'd rather have one God idea than a thousand good ideas."[6] Here is the amazing thing: 2 Thessalonians 1:11 assures us that not only do our good ideas come from God, but when we act in faith on those ideas, God engages His energy in bringing them about in ways that matter. "We … pray that our God will make you fit for what he's called you to be, pray that he'll fill your good ideas and acts of faith with his own energy so that it all amounts to something" (2 Thess 1:11). kingdom impact begins with ideas given to us by God in the quiet place.

Jesus Practiced Solitude

Jesus lived out these rhythms, regularly seeking a solitary place to be alone with the Father. Throughout His earthly ministry of teaching, healing, performing miracles, and making disciples, Jesus modeled a life of solitude (See Matt 4:1-11; 14:23; 17:1-9; Mark 1:35; Luke 5:16; 6:12). We are invited to follow His example.

In Mark 6, Jesus shows us that solitude was not an afterthought but a primary responsibility for leaders that provides a cadence to make life in ministry sustainable. After a season of success, with yet more and more people pressing in, Jesus immediately instructed His disciples, "Come away to a deserted place all by yourselves and rest a while" (Mark 6:31). Jesus seems more concerned with rhythms that will sustain His disciples in future ministry than in the success of the past.

It is crucial that we cease at times
from that which is necessary.

Before sending His followers into the next phase of ministry, Jesus called them to disengage. This implication for us is that we must serve others from a place of strength and not depletion. It is crucial that we cease at times from that which is necessary.

Scripture offers amazing accounts of solitude when God was most active:

- Moses was alone in the wilderness when God showed up (Exod 3:1-5).
- Gideon was by himself when commissioned to save Israel (Judg 6:11).
- Elijah was alone in despair when the Lord came to him in a gentle whisper (1 Kgs 19:12).
- Jesus often pulled away to be alone with His Father (Matt 4:1-11; 14:23; Mark 1:32-39; 6:46; Luke 5:15-16; 6:12-19).
- Cornelius was by himself praying when the Angel of the Lord came to him (Acts 10:1-4).
- No one was with Peter on the housetop when he was called to the Gentiles (Acts 10:9-28).

- John wrote the Book of Revelation alone on an island (Rev 1:9).

For the Sake of the World

The practice of solitude is not merely self-indulgent exercises for those times when an overcrowded soul needs a little time to itself. They are a beginning place, for sure but not the goal. Solitude ceases to solely provide a quiet place or inactivity but become an inner quality of our hearts that we carry within as we reenter our world of busyness. In the end, solitude becomes a way of loving others, those we serve and those who are our neighbors. We now possess an internal reality of peace, compassion, and mercy available to those we soon encounter that we would not have otherwise, that propels us to courage and unreserved engagement with a broken world.

Showing Up Counts

I won't give you "Five Easy Steps to Solitude." We love formulas so that we can control that space to our liking, and in doing so, miss the whole point. I will tell you that it takes time to feel comfortable with solitude. It takes time to train ourselves not to require that 'something' happen and give up our need to control that space or accomplish something. It takes time to push beyond the distractions and noises of our minds.

The key is to give ourselves the chance. We need not have *ah-ha* moments. Just showing up day after day, we can have the confidence that a shift is taking place in our souls, even if we are unaware of it. For the most part, stopping and quieting oneself involves sheer discipline. However, even when nothing seems to be happening, and when our times of solitude are fraught with distractions, inner restlessness, preoccupations, boredom, or personal anxieties, we remind ourselves that just being with Jesus is transformational.

Just showing up day after day, we can have the confidence that a shift is taking place in our souls, even if we are unaware of it.

Only through a crisis did I realize the full extent of how solitude shaped my life.

"Mom! He's in our lane!"

Even before my daughter screamed those words, I saw a car crossing into our lane of traffic. We were traveling the sixty-mph speed limit on a two-lane country road.

"I know, I see him," were all the words I could get out.

The mind is an amazing thing. In the few seconds before impact, I assessed all the options. I thought about hitting my brakes but knew there was a semi-truck following too close. We would be fatally smashed from behind. I couldn't swerve left into the long line of oncoming traffic. That didn't seem like a great option either. We had nowhere to go. I knew a collision was evitable. I remember thinking, I don't know how this is going to end. Honestly, given the options, I didn't think it would end well.

I watched our vehicles speed straight toward each other. Collision was inevitable. Just before impact, I closed my eyes. It wasn't how I always thought I would close my eyes in such a situation. I didn't squeeze them tightly shut, covering them with my hands, and grimacing my face like I do at a scary movie. Instead, I closed my eyes in the same way I do every morning in my big brown, over-stuffed chair. Slowly. Worshipfully. Peacefully. Hopefully. In that split second, my mind was taken back to that leather chair where I shut out all the other distractions and allow my soul to commune with God every morning. In that dire moment, I experienced the same Presence who meets me in the daily quiet place.

I don't remember hearing shattering glass or the sound of crunching metal. I don't remember the impact or coming to a stop. When I slowly opened my eyes, I expected to see my den, stacks of books, and the pictures of my family. What I saw was a completely demolished van, shattered windows, and an engine that appeared missing. Cars had stopped. People were gathering to see if we were okay. Other than a few bruises we were miraculously alive. Jesus saved our lives that day. Yet, similarly, he was saving my soul through solitude in my big brown chair.

Psalm 16:8 says, "I have kept the Lord ever before me; because he is at my right hand, I will not be shaken." That truth became not just a nice saying on a coffee mug but a reality. In those daily, quiet encounters with Jesus, divine formation and activity were going on beneath my consciousness. Those daily moments of 'showing up' forged an anchor in my soul that helped keep me in the storm.

Don't wait for a crisis. By then it is too late
to cultivate a steady heart.

For many of us, not until we hit some 'wall' do we consider the importance of time with God. Unfortunately, we often don't feel any need for stopping until we run out of gas, or life becomes unmanageable and forces us involuntarily into a place of rest. Life has a way of sideswiping us. Don't wait for a crisis. By then it is too late to cultivate a steady heart. How much better to embrace silence and solitude on your terms than when life forces you to stop.

I invite you to spend unhurried, uncluttered, and spacious time with Jesus. Take such a moment now with no agenda, and nothing to accomplish. Just be. Leave behind any hopes of discovering a marvelous strategy for fixing your life or your ministry. Simply sit quietly and alone with Jesus. Listen carefully for His loving voice. Embrace fully all He desires to do in you as you sit quietly and patiently before Him. Showing up counts. It is one more way of keeping company with Jesus.

Sabbath: Rest for Run Away Souls

"Sabbath is the one commandment we brag about breaking." — Author unknown

"Sabbath is that uncluttered time and space in which we can distance ourselves from our own activities enough to see what God is doing."[7]

"When was the last time you turned it off?" Turning off my laptop is always the 'go-to' advice my husband smugly gives me when my laptop is not behaving as it should. Surprisingly, unplugging always seems to work. Once, my laptop indicated, "Storage is full." I took it to an Apple store to see how I could increase its hard drive capacity. The polite, twenty-something technician took my laptop and thirty seconds later handed it back to me. "There, it's fixed. You now have plenty of storage." I fumbled, "What did you do?" "I just emptied the trash," he answered. All my laptop needed to work properly was to get rid of the useless files that took up precious space.

To whiz through our obligations without time for a single, mindful breath has become the model of success. Our souls, minds, and bodies were never created for unceasing activity or with the ability to bear the unrelenting pace of life and ministry. To ignore human limits leaves us emotionally, physically, and spiritually depleted.

Our Lives Are in Danger

Tragically, we often don't recognize this desperate state as we step into a place of leadership. Yet, this is our undoing. As Wayne Muller laments,

> Our culture invariably supposes that action and accomplishment are better than rest, that doing something … anything …is better than doing nothing. Because of our desire to succeed, to meet these ever-growing expectations, we do not rest. Because we do not rest, we lose our way. We miss the compass points that would show us where to go, we bypass the nourishment that would give us succor. We miss the quiet that would give us wisdom. We miss the joy and love born of effortless delight. Poisoned by this hypnotic belief that good things come only through unceasing determination and tireless effort, we can never truly rest. And … for want of rest, our lives are in danger.[8]

In a culture that values ceaseless activity, Jesus shows us another way.

Have you ever noticed the jerky movements of a pigeon's head when it walks? (I know that question has been on your top ten questions of the week.) Pigeons' eyes cannot focus as quickly as ours. The 'nodding' is a way of making the head stay still long enough to allow the eyes to 'catch up' and focus. We share the pigeon's dilemma: we cannot focus while on the run.

The literal meaning of Sabbath in Hebrew is "Stop it. Quit." Pause for a minute and read those words with the urgency with which they were intended: "STOP! QUIT!" It can also mean to catch our breath. I like that. In a leadership culture of hurry, the need to embrace a different rhythm from the urgency of our days. Intentional rest should top our calendar list as essential.

Sabbath is not simply a day off, an escape, or a day to binge-watch on Netflix. Neither is Sabbath merely an opportunity to 'recharge our battery' so we can get productive again. If that were true, we would only observe Sabbath when we feel depleted. Most of the time, we tell ourselves we are fine. We don't see the need for a holy pause.

Most of the time, we tell ourselves
we are fine.
We don't see the need
for a holy pause.

Contrasted against the pace and struggles of the other six days, Sabbath stands out as a holy day, a separate and distinct day from the others. Note Exodus 20:8:

> Remember to observe the Sabbath day by keeping it holy. Six days a week are set apart for your daily duties and regular work, but the seventh day is a day of rest dedicated to the Lord your God. On that day, no one in your household may do any kind of work, which includes you, your sons and daughters, your male and female servants, your livestock and any foreigners living among you, for in six days, the Lord made the heavens, the earth, the sea and everything in them, then He rested on the seventh day. That is why the Lord blessed the seventh day and set it apart as holy.

Dan Allender explains, "Holy simply means set aside, not lost in the sea of everything else."[9] It has to do with setting aside a day in which we live differently, and we experience life differently. It means setting apart time that makes it distinctive from our ordinary patterns of relating to the world.

A Rhythm of Rest

When my son attended our local community college, one of his core classes was World History. Geek that I am, I was flipping through the pages of his *World History and Cultures* textbook, and I happened upon a reference to the French Revolution, and this paragraph caught my eye:

> To remove any remnant of religion from government, the Convention introduced a new calendar which removed Sundays, Easter, Christmas, and all other religious holidays. To avoid dating history by the birth of Christ, they declared the year 1792 to be the beginning of the Republic. Months were renamed, and weeks were declared to be ten days long rather than seven. (They were named "Decades," with the tenth day of each day taking the place of Sunday.) It is said that people and even horses[10] were physically unable to cope with ignoring God's law of one day of rest in every seven. The system was shortly abandoned as unworkable.[11]

Rest was never meant to be a luxury. Rest is a necessity—one we often ignore.

Sometimes ministry leaders acknowledge, in a bragging kind-of-way, "I haven't taken a vacation in twelve years!" There is nothing noble in that. When we are unable to stop or say "no" to the demands of others, our actions may seem heroic to ourselves, but this messiah complex prevents us from realizing our limitations. We create an environment that makes it difficult to admit our humanity. We act as though we are rescuers rather than coworkers with God and His kingdom purposes. The problem is that there will always be those in need of rescuing. If ministry begins with the needs of people, there is a never-ending supply.

We act as though we are rescuers rather than coworkers with God and His kingdom purposes.

God tied the Sabbath to freedom from slavery. Recorded in Deuteronomy 5:12-15: "Don't ever forget that you were slaves in Egypt and that God, your God, got you out of there in a powerful show of strength. That's why God, your God, commands you to observe the day of Sabbath rest." Sabbath is an act of freedom for a free person has control over their time. Only slaves don't rest. Whenever I struggle with taking a Sabbath, I remind myself of this truth.

I was leading a retreat on these practices of leadership. Participants were instructed to observe a weekly Sabbath day for a month. When we gathered again a month later, I asked about their experience of practicing Sabbath. Most shared how difficult it was to 'spend' a day not working. The challenge of actually stopping and disengaging caused surprised frustration. One honest leader observed, "I didn't practice it because I didn't earn it."

We have this idea that when everything is done, it means we have worked hard; then we deserve to rest. Rest, we assume is our reward for working hard and completing a task. Yet, as Wayne Muller wisely instructs, "We stop because it is time to stop. Sabbath requires surrender. If we only stop when we are finished [our emails, our projects], we will never stop—because our work is never completely done."[12] If we refuse to rest until we are finished, we will never rest until we die or until our work kills us.

Researchers have come up with a term for the stressed-out feeling that there's never enough time for what we want to do. They call it "time famine." Mark Buchanan offers this alternative: "Sabbath liberates us from the need to be finished."[13] Practicing Sabbath resides in our theological conviction that God is the One who is already creatively and redemptively at work building His Church.

This is the test of Sabbath-keeping: the ability to rest in God's providence and creative activity doing what only He can do.

If we assume that the success of our ministry rests squarely on our abilities, strengths, and ingenuity, we won't rest. We can't risk everything falling apart. We won't dare risk taking a Sabbath. This is the test of Sabbath-keeping: the ability to rest in God's providence and creative activity doing what only He can do.

An Organizing Principle

Jesus reiterates Sabbath as a sheer gift—His gift to our frantic souls, our exhausted bodies, and our relationships with others. It is a gift that enables us to enjoy God and those we love. It is not something to which one must slavishly conform. In six recorded clashes with Jesus and the religious leaders over Sabbath-keeping, Jesus did not dispute the significance of the Sabbath. Instead, He addressed appropriate behavior and embraced its qualities. Jesus elevated the spirit or intention of the Sabbath above the letter of the Mosaic Law of Sabbath of dutiful rituals and rules.

Andy Crouch suggests that Sabbath not be just one day a week. It is intended to be an organizing principle in our lives. Crouch suggests a simple, minimal pattern of Sabbath: "We choose to turn off our devices not just one day a week but also one hour (or more) each day and one week (or more) every year."[14] Some leaders have the privilege of going on a sabbatical. Sabbaticals are an extended period granted for spiritual renewal and restoration. However, the spaciousness, benefits, and gains of sabbaticals are lost if leaders return to the same frenzied rhythms of busyness. Sabbath, as an organizing principle, becomes an intentional way of living that marks all of our days.

Because Sunday is a workday, my husband and I observe a weekly Friday Sabbath. (You might take a different day.) We try, not always successfully, to disconnect from technology except to talk to our kids. We sleep in. My husband cooks a big breakfast. I light two candles representing rest and freedom. We pray together. We go for a walk. We leisurely enjoy coffee on our deck. We read for enjoyment. We eat our way through the local Farmer's Market or meet our kids or friends for lunch. I often spend time in my garden, celebrating new growth or the promise of harvest, and appreciating the bees "who are doing such a good job" of pollination (as my granddaughter says). I probably pick a few weeds. I love picking weeds. Weird, I know. No, don't ask me to come pick yours. My garden is a source of delight, relaxation, and a perfect complement to my Sabbath.

My husband and I guard our Sabbath day closely, but still there are times when our Sabbath gets absorbed in work-ish things. We don't do it perfectly, and we are okay with that. We are reminded that we are not slaves to the Sabbath. However, we must be on guard that we do not get caught up in excuses to the detriment of our Sabbath commitment.

What might Sabbath look like for you? Feel free to craft it as you wish, making sure it is life-giving. Don't do it out of guilt but as an act of freedom and rest.

Ignoring Our Limits

Every year our four adult kids, spouses, and our ten grandchildren gather at our home for a traditional Fourth of July barbeque. When we all come together, I call it my Wild, Crazy, Wonderful. Of the ten grandchildren, nine are ages seven and under. This means there is always someone sleeping, someone crying, and something is breaking. As I anticipate everyone coming home, I spend long days cleaning, grocery shopping, cooking, clearing my emails, and working in the yard. It is usually a hot week with temperatures bumping a hundred degrees. We have extra bedrooms, so they stay with us, filling our bedrooms with suitcases, portable cribs, and the kind of toys you step on in the middle of the night.

Fourth of July fell on a weekend one year. That Sunday my husband and I left home early to make final preparations for our church services. Everyone else would meet us there. At the conclusion of worship, it struck me that somehow, after standing through four songs, I had not sung a single word. Like driving a car and not remembering how you got from one place to another, I had somehow not been present to the last twenty minutes of the service.

Strange, I thought. Unreflectively, I shook it off and after the service greeted people in the lobby. (Later, they commented on how I was not my bubbly self. "You were not all there," commented one friend.) My daughter came up and asked me where we were going for lunch. While I heard her words, I could not focus well enough to formulate an answer. She pressed me but impatiently walked away when I could not make a decision. Someone else had to make the lunch decision.

At home later that afternoon, my three-year-old granddaughter wanted to eat blueberries growing in the far corner of our property. "Carry me, Grandma," she insisted. I picked her up, but the extreme temperature and my sapped energy forced me to put her down. Then she wanted to pet my daughter's horse in the pasture next to our house. Not to disappoint, I walked her to the barn and offered our horse an apple and a nose rub.

The next thing I remember is staring up at two medics in an ambulance. They were taking my blood pressure and asking me the name of the president of the United States. At least I got that right! I asked the medics what happened.

"You had a seizure," they answered.

"Serious?" I whispered in disbelief.

I had no family or medical history of seizures and was in excellent health. I rode to the hospital in disbelief. My family met me there. My poor husband was frantic while my kids chided me for downplaying my 'episode.' The doctor prodded me with questions. "What do you do?" he asked.

We think our tireless efforts are what will make us successful, but what they actually do is make us sick.

"Well, I am on staff at a large church, I run an LLC, I lead other upper-level leaders in various capacities, I am a life coach, oh, I am in a doctoral program." Someone had asked me not long before that episode how I was managing it all. "I think I am balancing everything pretty good." Obviously, I wasn't. The doctor concluded that my seizure was brought on by dehydration, exhaustion, and stress. Go figure.

Because many of us are competent and high-capacity people, we soldier on, often oblivious to what is happening in our souls and bodies. We deny the weight we carry. We assume we are somehow exempt from the consequences of ignoring our limits.

Our bodies often reflect what's going on inside us. We may experience unexplainable physical illnesses like muscle tension, high blood pressure, lethargy, stomach aches and headaches. Our bodies carry the weight of our anxious souls. Like the idiot lights in our cars, our bodies signal to us that all is not well. As we may do with our car's signals, we can choose to ignore our physical symptoms and internal warnings. It has been said, "If we don't take a Sabbath, our bodies will take it for us."[15] My dangerous tendency to think I could remain untouched by the load and pressures I carried may be more common than we think. Our out-of-control activism comes at a high price. We think our tireless efforts are what will make us successful, but what they actually do is make us sick.

Interestingly, what was most affected by my lack of rest and self-care was my ability to pay attention.

That Sunday, I completely missed my body's faithful warning signals. They went unheeded in my complete and utter lack of self-awareness. I unwittingly lost the ability to worship or focus my thoughts. I lost my ability to notice rumblings beneath the surface of my life. I lost the capacity to be present to myself and others. Interestingly, *what was most affected by my lack of rest and self-care was my ability to pay attention.*

Instead of simply responding to all the needs of people and demands of ministry, what if we begin at some other point? What would it look like if we serve from a place of strength and a more spacious perspective? What if what people needed most from us is not more work, but more rest? What if that is what you and I also need most today?

9

Present to Self: Listen to Your Life

"Self-reflective work is the work
of personal integration."[1]

I stood in the front row at the ladies' retreat with my eyes closed and hands raised. The room was alive with a sense of God's presence as the worship team powerfully sang, "Savior, He can move the mountains, our God is mighty to save; mighty to save!" My mind sorted through all of the 'mountains' in my life that I needed God to move. My heart cried for God's intervention and His wonder-working ways. With my arms still raised, I heard God speak. Although spoken in a noise-filled environment, His voice was clear and gentle, "Gail. You are that mountain." Although startled by His voice, I wasn't surprised by His words. Neither was His voice one of condemnation or shame; it felt like yet another invitation to wholeness.

My heart, not my circumstances,
needed a mighty Savior.

I am mindful that many of my prayers appeal for God to act in my circumstances. I want deliverance. I want mountains moved. I want to be saved from how things are, but too often I don't pray for God to act *in me*. As soon as I heard those words, I knew that healing from my brokenness was my deliverance. My heart, not my circumstances, needed a mighty Savior.

If I have learned anything in my walk with God, it is that my wounded soul is deeply in need of healing. What is present under the surface of my life should not be ignored. As long as I can remember, I have lived with an awareness of my woundedness. And as long as I can remember, I have pursued God's work of healing and wholeness. Some people live and die in their woundedness. I don't want to be one of them. Owning my story with all of its brokenness and pain and living vulnerably is extremely hard but not nearly as difficult as spending my life running from it. There was still so much more of me that needed surrendering. And now before me was yet another invitation to a new work of grace. I smiled and answered, "Let's do this."

The focus of chapters 9 and 10 will be the emotional life of the leader—that part of our lives that often remains hidden yet has a way of running our lives and ultimately forming the place from which we minister. A necessary component of our well-being and effective ministry must include a willingness to pay careful attention to the state of our hearts and to the unexamined inner dynamics that drive us. We must be willing to look at our hidden compulsions, fears, and faulty patterns of thinking.

A Fundamental Pastoral Practice

Do you remember Jesus's instructions in Mark 12:29-30? Give your biggest attention to the things that matter most. The self is included in that. Self-examination is one of the most misunderstood and underused spiritual practice. Yet, historically, it formed the bedrock in the spiritual life and habits of the Church. Far from being antisocial or narcissistic, looking more carefully at the role the inner life plays in the life of a leader emerges as a fundamental pastoral practice for a leader who leads from a place of authenticity, wholeness, and flourishing. Ruth Haley Barton articulates, "Spiritual leadership emerges from our willingness to stay involved with our own soul."[2] Leading in a distracted culture requires practices which allow enough space and reflection to ask probing question such as, "How is my life unfolding?" or "Is this how I want to live?" Seth Richardson notes, "In a world where the conditions that supported long-held assumptions about church and leadership are shifting, I'm convinced that asking 'what is going on?' is not only necessary for finding your bearings in the midst of disorientation, it is a fundamental pastoral practice."[3]

"I'm convinced that asking 'what is going on?' is not only necessary for finding your bearings in the midst of disorientation, it is a fundamental pastoral practice."

John Piper, high profile author and pastor of Bethlehem Baptist Church announced he was taking an eight-month unexpected leave of absence from public ministry, noting,

> I see several species of pride in my soul that, while they may not rise to the level of disqualifying me for ministry, grieve me, and have taken a toll on my relationship with [my wife] Noël and others who are dear to me. How do I apologize to you, not for a specific deed, but for ongoing character flaws, and their effects on everybody?[4]

Later he wrote an article titled, "Pastor, Know Thy Self":

> Everyone should do this for his own soul. Pastors, you will know your people's souls best by knowing your own. So try to be ruthlessly honest with yourself. The key here is not professionalism. The best soul-searcher

> and the best counselor may have no letters after their names. The key is brutal, broken vulnerability and honesty, sustained by pleas for mercy, and soaked in the riches of Scripture—both its warnings and its wonders.[5]

Piper appeals to us to consider the importance of facing ourselves. His advice is sound and doesn't let us off the hook by ignoring or dismissing our brokenness. When we become aware of our brokenness, rather than do the hard work of facing our lives, the temptation may be to lean toward spiritualizing everything. I heard a pastor preach about depression: "We just need to get back to the Word!" Yes, to know ourselves requires a trusted reliance on God's Word. We also need an honest self-awareness that many of the struggles and obstacles we face are psychological in nature. Todd Wilson, president and co-founder and of the Center for Pastor Theologians, explains,

> Many forms of evangelical spirituality fail to foster integration. We prioritize doctrinal instruction and moral development, but we neglect psychological healing. We emphasize the cultivation of character, but we overlook our psychological compulsions, fixations, and emotional reactivity. This type of spirituality will breed disintegrated pastors whose ministries will sooner or later disintegrate around them.[6]

One of the great dangers in ministry is the capacity for hiddenness. Most people at our church see me just once a week, for an hour or so, when I am in control of what I want them to see. Even if I am being vulnerable or authentic, I am doing so intentionally. However, it is naive and self-deceptive to I think I could hide my brokenness. Sooner or later disheartening cracks in my personality come out, usually in unexpected ways.

Our disintegration eventually pours over into the lives of those we serve, as Merton warns:

> He who attempts to act and do things for others or for the world without deepening his own self-understanding, freedom, integrity, and capacity to love, will not have anything to give others. He will communicate to them nothing but the contagion of his own obsessions, his aggressiveness, his ego-centered ambitions.[7]

Our disintegration eventually pours over into the lives of those we serve.

Our leadership becomes harmful when our brokenness remains unresolved.

Coming to Grips with Our Brokenness

An important component of authentic leadership is the necessity to remain real and open to what is true about us—the real us. Seeing ourselves as we really are can be scary. Many of us fear giving attention to the voices that call us worthless and unlovable. However, personal faithfulness for leaders must include a courageous readiness to not assume that our lives are as they appear. Authentic leadership must also include a profound willingness to embrace and acknowledge our human condition with emotional honesty.

At one time, while working with a group of leaders I asked them to take a survey about their well-being as leaders. Here is how they responded when asked the following questions:

- How would you rate your spiritual well-being? Fifty-two percent responded, "very good" or "good." That means almost half—forty-eight percent—of leaders rated their spiritual health as not good.

- How would you rate your emotional health? Forty-eight percent rated it average or below average.
- Sixty-two percent do not take a daily quiet time.
- Ninety-five percent agreed with the statement, "I feel overwhelmed by the demands of life."
- Only twenty-six percent said that their current ministry work was significant and fulfilling. That means seventy-four percent of ministry leaders do not find their ministry important or meaningful.
- In response to the statement, "I often feel inadequate as a ministry leader," sixty-three percent either agreed or strongly agreed.
- In response to the statement, "I take time for self-reflection/examination," Forty-two percent disagreed or were undecided.

These leaders courageously revealed that ninety-five percent of them are overwhelmed.

These leaders courageously revealed that ninety-five percent of them are overwhelmed. They struggled with insignificance, inadequacy, instability, neglect, loss of introspection, and a sense of failure. It is my guess that, unknowingly, a sense of shame surrounded these feelings. As ministry leaders we understand the tension of our incongruency, knowing that what we preach is not always how we live. Pastor Stephen Woodworth aptly describes this dilemma:

> To one degree or another, every pastor feels the gnawing sense of their own hypocrisy. We are called to preach, week after week, about a vision of Christianity that we

> may not fully experience, a love from God we sometimes don't feel, prayer we don't practice, parenting and marriage advice we forget to employ in our own homes, forgiveness we struggle to give, and an identity in Christ in which we struggle to stay rooted.[8]

These statistics are concerning. Not paying attention to the impact that our work is having has its own consequences. The costs of an unexamined inner life are high. Of course, one of the worst misconceptions is that leaders should never struggle.

Leading in a VUCA World

Compounding to the struggles of our inner life is an outer world of increasing complexity and instability. As I write this, we are in the middle of a worldwide pandemic because of a virus called the novel coronavirus (COVID-19). Businesses, schools, and churches are closed. Local governing authorities have imposed mandatory "stay at home" orders and facemasks. Millions of jobs are lost, setting off an economic crisis. At the beginning of this crisis, people were panicking, grabbing for whatever made them feel safe and secure. Grocery store managers had to separate people fighting over water and toilet paper! Few people didn't feel somewhat anxious at this upheaval in their lives.

As leaders, we find ourselves confronted with continual and unprecedented cultural and global changes. Cultural norms are pushed far beyond expectations and comprehension. We struggle with an increasing inability to understand and lead in these uncertain and perilous times. Ministry is not what it used to be, and it is probably not what we thought we were signing up for.

The reality of instability and unpredictability within the leadership world can be described by an acronym called VUCA, which describes the situation when the external world is characterized as being essentially volatile, uncertain, complex, and ambiguous. Developed by Warren Bennis and Burt Nanus, it was first tested in the U.S. Army Military College in the 1990s. VUCA describes the changing nature of military intervention in modern warfare. It describes the unpredictable way a situation can escalate every quickly, the uncertainty people experience around every corner or with every person they meet, and the complex strategies and threats to safety unfolding in field situations such as Iraq and Afghanistan.

In other words, emotional development becomes an essential precursor to a more integrated leadership.

Few of us would deny that uncertainty, complexity, constant change, and ambiguity describes our days and our ability to lead. We lead in a VUCA world. It is difficult to keep up and to make sense of things, yet it is our new normal. Integrating VUCA realities into life and leadership goes beyond harnessing more organizational skills. As blogger Nick Ross offers,

> Greater complexity and ambiguity require greater interiority. The ability to reconcile the tension between a leader's external and inner worlds is fundamental to 21st-century leadership development. Put another way, the psychological health of the leader will be a key differentiator in coming years.[9]

In other words, emotional development becomes an essential precursor to a more integrated leadership.

Listen to Your Life

Unfortunately, some of us work and live with little self-reflection. We function without perspective or understanding why we do what we do. Think of how often we make the same mistakes, repeat the same harmful behavioral patterns, and react in ways that surprise even ourselves. If we are unfamiliar with our brokenness, our brokenness has complete autonomy in our lives. Only when we stop to reflect upon these experiences and extract their hidden insights do we open ourselves to the possibilities of real change. Someone has said that not facing the reality of our darkness and its sources is a really, really bad idea.

If we are unfamiliar with our brokenness,
our brokenness has complete
autonomy in our lives.

Emotional development. Self-examination. Self-reflection. We typically are not used to such inward introspection and probably not comfortable thinking about that. However, it is time to listen to your life. The Apostle Paul instructs, "Make a careful exploration of who you are and the work you have been given, and then sink yourself into that" (Gal 6:4-5). Deep self-awareness does not come about haphazardly, coincidentally, or naturally. Attentiveness to the condition of one's life requires deliberate intent, practiced focus, and a trained ability to remain present to what is most real about one's self, no matter how that reality unfolds.

It is vital to create a reliable pattern of living
that will serve you well.

Heading off unto the unknown with God is not for the faint of heart. The good news is it can become a place of discovery where our truest identity is formed. Consider the words of Psalm 51:6 (MSG), "What you're after is truth from the inside out.

Enter me, then; conceive a new, true life." Ultimately, we best minister from a place where we have nothing to defend, to prove, or compete against. It is vital to create a reliable pattern of living that will serve you well.

The False Self

There is a time of day every afternoon that I just dread. At 4:00 p.m. the afternoon light streams through the entire west side of my home, exposing it to the intense light of day. All the dust and dirt that has unsuspectedly accumulated is revealed in its disgusting glory. I am aghast at the unsightly mess, hoping no one stops by for a visit at that moment. My common response is to criticize myself for being such a sloppy housekeeper. I start to clean but then give up, frustrated by the enormity of the task. Often, I simply close the curtain and wait for the sun to go down, hoping I no longer notice it.

This false self is the person
we *wish* we were.
It is the constructed self
we want others to *think* we are.

We instinctively know there is part of us that we hide from others. For if they knew who (or what) we really are, we are certain and afraid that they would not like what they see. Everything within us wants to show our best 'pretend self.' This false self is the person we *wish* we were. It is the constructed self we want others to *think* we are. The illusion is achieved by an elaborate means of maintaining this illusion. The false self needs constant approval and behaves in ways we think guarantee us to be accepted, needed, and admired. The false self searches for some kind of significance by what we do, and "hustles for our worthiness by constantly performing, perfecting, pleasing and proving,"[10] The false self pretends all is well. The temptation to hang on to the false self is constant.

Shame makes us imagine God saying to us,
"You are such a disappointment."

Shame creates the false self. Shame is elusive, and we rarely mention it in leadership circles. However, it can feel like humiliation, embarrassment, or inadequacy. Shame's most basic message is, "I am not enough." "I am not pretty, talented, smart enough." "I wish I wasn't … (fill in the blank)." Shame is our inner critic constantly reminding us of our unworthiness. Shame makes us imagine God saying to us, "You are such a disappointment."

Ministry leadership is a fertile breeding ground for shame because so much of leadership is performance-based. We try to find significance by what we do, the title we hold, or what we own. We use busyness to convince us we are okay. The busier we are, the more important we may seem. We want to say, "Let me show you my calendar to prove my worth." Everyone is subject to shame—*everyone*. David Letterman, reflecting on the relationship between performance and self-worth, notes,

> Every night you're trying to prove your self-worth. It's like meeting your girlfriend's family for the first time. You want to be the absolute best, wittiest, smartest, most charming, best-smelling version of yourself. If I can make people enjoy the experience and have a higher regard for me when I'm finished, it makes me feel like an entire person. If I've come short of that, I'm not happy. How things go for me every night is how I feel about myself for the next 24 hours.[11]

Can you relate to that in ministry? Attendance, offering, video views, likes or shares: you check to make sure you are still okay. I am frustrated and disappointed that I still allow those things to determine how the rest of my day goes.

Jim Carrey, when accepting a Golden Globe award at the 2016 Golden Globes, said,

> And when I dream, I don't just dream any old dream. No sir. I dream about being a three-time Golden Globe-winning actor Jim Carrey. Because then I would be enough. It would finally be true. And I could stop this terrible search … for what I know ultimately won't fulfill me.[12]

Jim understood the false self's gnawing need to be enough.

What is our usual default response when we are shamed? Our first instinct is to self-protect. So, we hide, deny, and numb ourselves. We hide our wounded selves from others. Our self-protection exposes itself as blame, rationalizing, or defensiveness. The grandson of one of my friends doesn't like being left in the church nursery. So, he keeps his eyes closed for several minutes after being dropped off, hoping that if he doesn't see it, it's not real. Denial does not make shame go away.

I choose to trust that there is
some truth in our emotions.

More subtle ways of dealing with shame include the need to rescue others, the need to be liked, or the unwillingness to stop working. It may involve isolation, rigidity, or perfectionism, but eventually our wounded selves splatter across our lives. We may have outbursts of anger, jealousy, resentment, or bitterness. Brene Brown offers a critical insight that we are unable to selectively numb our emotions. We cannot selectively numb the bad stuff like shame, guilt, grief, fear, and disappointment. When we numb, we also anesthetize joy, gratitude, and happiness—all the things that make life good.[13] This is huge. I would rather choose the bad with the good than go through life feeling nothing. That is no way to live. In fact, you are not really living at all.

Emotions tell you what's going on in your life. I know that emotions must not be given free rein in our lives and should come under scrutiny, but I choose to trust that there is some truth in our emotions. Scripture is replete with emotion. The Psalms record the whole gamut of human passions and frustration, from the highest highs to the lowest lows. Moses was stubborn. He got angry … a lot. David danced and bitterly mourned. Elijah was in the deepest of despair and emotionally spent. Gideon was afraid. Mary rejoiced. Paul expressed gratitude, despair, and deep love. Thomas doubted. James and John were arrogant and proud. And Jesus wept.

People found God in each of these places. God meets you in your emotions, for they tell you what's going on inside and what truly matters to you. Dan Allender and Tremper Longman offer this insightful point: "Listening to our emotions ushers us into reality. And reality is where we meet God."[14] To ignore your emotions keeps you guarded and defensive. You tuck your true self away and cut yourself off from everything that would bring refreshment. You live a shadow of life and deny those things that make you fully human.

Leading from Weakness

I subscribe to a lot of leadership blogs and newsletters. While most are inspiring, challenging, and helpful, sometimes it becomes wearying to read about all the success strategies. "5 Things Successful Leaders Do." "Top Strategies for …" "Critical Elements Every Leader Must …" I have to admit, my life is organized, and most often my days are ordered in successful ways. There is something about leading from a place of strength that appeals to me. Yet more times than I like to admit, I feel equally fraught with feelings of inadequacy and incompetence. I worry I will be found wanting among all the leadership gurus.

More times than I like to admit,
I feel equally fraught with
feelings of inadequacy
and incompetence.

A while ago, I chatted with a newcomer to our church. She commented that when she was on the leadership team at her previous church, it was difficult to continually 'stay strong,' to always 'have it all together,' and to always remain upbeat. I had a hunch it was also exhausting.

"I try to lead from a different place," I responded. "I endeavor to lead from my brokenness." She did not try to hide her shock. I don't think she had ever thought of this before.

I am struck with the thought that most often my most authentic ministry comes from my brokenness, not my strengths. I don't disregard the skills and talents given me; they serve me well, but in the end, I am fully aware that leading from a place of sufficiency often becomes a way of self-protecting (so others don't see how afraid I am), leaves my activist ego intact, and, ultimately, denies what is most human about me: my shared brokenness.

Embracing our brokenness requires humility and a willingness to admit we are still on a journey to healing. This means we are allowed to be human again. People seek leaders who are approachable, transparent, and real. They don't want a superhuman leader. They want one who struggles like they do and who can still lead them through uncertainty and messiness with flexibility, grace, and a bit of playfulness. Leading from weakness permits others to be vulnerable and share their fears. This creates a church culture where everyone can be imperfect but still deeply loved and greatly valued by others and God.

This means we are allowed
to be human again.

The idea of embracing one's weakness feels counterintuitive. However, in Scripture it is weakness that tips God's hand. We assume that the grace of God enhances our weakness, but perhaps we should also view grace as the strength of God that is expressed through our weakness. Paul's language is, "When I am weak, then I am strong" (2 Cor 12:10). The "when" and the "then" are concurrent, not consecutive. In the place of felt weakness I become more fully aware of the grace of Christ enabling and energizing power that guides my thoughts, my words, and my steps. In other words, our struggles and weakness are the very things that allow us to experience grace.

Our struggles and weakness are the very things
that allow us to experience grace.

Strength in weakness requires a dependency to receive something outside oneself. Weakness is not the end of our leadership, although it can feel that way; rather, it is simply the beginning of something new. The good news is that this is not an either/or situation. We can and should flourish in our gifts, all the while knowing that in God's kingdom our wounds are just as transformative as our strengths.

Our Healing Begins

I have every right to be a mess. My mother carried the wounds of this world and struggled with mental health all her life. She used alcohol to self-medicate so she could get up every morning and work to provide for her three children. My two siblings and I are each ten months apart. I was the youngest, which means that my mother, separated from my father just after I was born, had three children under the age of two. Although she remarried four more times, she spent most of her adult life as a single mother.

Being raised in an irreligious, alcoholic, abusive, and divorced home has shaped me in profound ways. The mantra of Adult Children of Alcoholics (ACoA) is, "Don't talk. Don't trust. Don't feel." You can imagine how these things play out in my real life. I brought these ingrained patterns and rhythms of relating and living into my marriage and my ministry.

I am well acquainted with my false self. Being an ACoA was an imposed identity, not the true self God had in mind when He created me. Facing my wounds, embracing my belovedness, and offering my broken self to the redemptive work of the Holy Spirit, every day, I see more and more of my real self shining through. By God's grace, I am not who I was. The Christian life has never been about being perfect or striving to attain perfection. Never. It has always been about a daily life-long journey of keeping company with Jesus. Simply by being with Him, we experience ongoing transformation. In that case, I figure I am right on target.

Showing my broken self has not always been easy in the church setting, especially as a leader. Too often the church has not been a safe place to let that broken self be seen. What would they think of me? How can they follow a leader who is far from perfect? What if we preached that the Christian journey is about *becoming* instead of having arrived? How much grace would be extended to others from those in need of grace themselves? What if we could show them what it means to be far from complete but still in communion with God?

For too, too long we have lived inauthentic to the reality of Christ, by masking our broken places as if we were the only ones, or as if denying our brokenness somehow kept us "holy."

As leaders, we are called to cultivate faith communities that become hospitals where wounded souls—including ours—find healing with other wounded souls. It is time to see ourselves as the fellowship of the broken. For too, too long we have lived inauthentic to the reality of Christ, by masking our broken places as if we were the only ones, or as if denying our brokenness somehow kept us 'holy.' But what we have denied is our humanness, the power of the Cross, the love of Christ, and the grace we so desperately need.

Weariness, sadness, loss, joy, courage … all make us "glorious ruins,"[15] but only when we embrace all of life and make space for grief, sadness, weariness, joy, or courage, do we give room for the souls to be heard. Only then can our healing begin.

10

Practicing Self-Awareness

"A dangerous leader is one that has great familiarity with their skills and gifts but cursory knowledge of their inner brokenness."[1]

"Of all the characteristics essential for leadership of modern organizations, I believe the most important is self-awareness. And it is only through assiduous attention to the inner life that such knowledge can grow."[2]

As we move into the practices of self-examination, we need to admit our brokenness and remain fully aware of what still lies within us. So much of our wounded selves still remains unknown to us on a conscious level. The worst thing we can do is to think that we can whip ourselves into shape on our own. Remember, our growth in self-knowledge is not to condemn us. The more self-aware we become, the more we grow in awareness of our need for God's grace. The more we become aware of God's grace, the more we can willingly offer our broken selves to the good work of grace. In other words, only after our brokenness comes to light can we offer our brokenness to God and receive healing. This breaks off any temptation to permit ourselves to live at surface level. When we finally stop pretending all is well, our brokenness can become redemptive.

Transformation is God's process of recreating our very selves. We receive it as a gift. Surrendering to this boundless and redemptive work of the Holy Spirit releases the fullness of Christ in us. Unfortunately, often we prefer rescue to redemption. We focus on our brokenness as a problem to be fixed rather than as a place where God is already present.

> Only after our brokenness comes to light can we offer our brokenness to God and receive healing.

So, what practices assist us in self-awareness and give the help we need to process our still-unfinished self without hardening or closing ourselves off or falling into the trap of self-deception? What practices assist us to remain faithful to truth, embrace vulnerability, be distinguished by humility, and stay open to change and redemption? Let's begin!

The Prayer of Examen

For centuries, Christians engaged in the Prayer of Examen as a means of increased awareness of God's activity, as well as a heightened self-awareness before God in the events of daily life. The goal in the Prayer of Examen, often referred to as "the practice of noticing,"[3] involves reviewing one's day, in the presence of God, to observe and discern the motives and inner realities that may otherwise go unnoticed.

How was God alive, active, and working in my life today? Examen is a tenacious look for that. With the fast pace of ministry and no intentional practice of self-awareness, we can remain blind to the shadow side of our lives. Examen creates space for reflection of the graces, large and seemingly insignificant, that have marked our day. Psalm 18:21 gives us our cue: "Every day I review the way he works" (MSG).

Examen helps us pause long enough, as John Baillie points out, to "ponder the pattern my life is weaving."[4] In short, the Prayer of Examen is a discipline to stay awake to our lives. As Smith explains, "Examen is a practice for paying attention to your life: reflect on God's presence; review your day in a spirit of gratitude; become aware of your emotions before God; pray over one feature of your day; and then intentionally look forward to tomorrow."[5]

The Prayer of Examen is a discipline
to stay awake to our lives.

The Prayer of Examen involves reviewing your day using a variety of questions:

1. Where have you noticed God's presence in your life today? Here are some other helpful questions that will lead you to personal reflection and self-discovery:

    - Where was God in this situation?
    - What Scripture came to mind throughout my day?
    - How did I sense God leading me?
    - What led me toward God?"

2. Where have you missed God's presence in your life today?
   "Let us test and examine our ways, and return to the Lord" (Lam 3:40). In the safety of God's love, you can deal honestly about what is most real about you. "Only under God's steady gaze of love are we able to find the healing and restoration we so desperately need."[6] Ask God to reveal to you the events and patterns of the day that did not lead to love and freedom in Christ (such as

anger, pride, jealousy, and anxiety). Some helpful questions you might ask:

- What kept me from noticing God's presence today?
- What was motivating my response or action?
- What unresolved or undetected inner brokenness still drives me?
- In what ways did I self-protect, deny, hide, or numb myself from others?

The Prayer of Examen, when used regularly, keeps you from merely floating through your spiritual life and remaining at the mercy of your drivenness. The Examen allows you to notice all the ways you have ignored this great work of grace or have been distracted or indifferent to it. Ultimately, the Prayer of Examen allows you to keep in step in the lively dance of redemption.

Telling Your Story

Our faith is more than an individual pursuit, possession, or process. The integrated life remains a shared journey. We must not only be willing to grow in self-awareness but also allow our lives to remain open for exposure in relationships of safety and empathy. God exists, relationally, within the community of the Godhead. Thus, we who share His image are created for relationship. Neurologically, we need each other. Neuropsychiatrist Siegel explains, "The brain is a social organ, and our relationships with one another are not a luxury but an essential nutrient for our survival."[7]

We are wired for connection. It is in our biology, and it is in connecting that we flourish. In other words, community is redemptive, relationships matter, and ministry leaders are no exception to this truth.

It is difficult for ministry leaders to embrace community. We resist community because it requires us to be vulnerable and disclosing. It is challenging to remain vulnerable in relationships when we spend so much energy helping others with their weaknesses while meticulously hiding our feelings of inadequacy and unworthiness. We can put a great deal of energy into maintaining our image. So, we hide our motives, fears, sin, shame, and weaknesses from others. Shame loves secrecy. Shame makes us hide or bury our story.

In fact, the end game of shame is always isolation. Relational isolation is a significant problem among ministry leaders. As Shelly Trebesch states, "… 95% of all leaders go through isolation."[8] Social scientists note that relational isolation, and the loneliness it creates, is now equally as bad for health as obesity or smoking. Statistics also tell us that isolated pastors are more susceptible to sadness, loneliness, anxiety, stress; discouragement, and temptation. You might secretly be nodding your head in agreement.

We can't experience wholeness alone.

Chuck DeGroat assesses the essential need for community: "Our divided hearts cannot heal in a vacuum."[9] We can't experience wholeness alone. Alone has left us exhausted, leading hidden lives and at the mercy of the false self. K. J. Ramsey notes,

> We become resilient not by denying the reality of brokenness or our feelings of vulnerability and shame but by naming them within relationships of safety and empathy. When we create space to lament and to tell our

> stories in the context of empathy and safety, our brains are rewired toward health.[10]

Redemptive relationships can be built, however, only if we are willing to remain transparent, vulnerable, and authentic. We need more than an accountability partner. It is not about reporting in; it is about being known. As Dr. Lissa Rankin affirms telling your story because "being witnessed with loving attention by others who care—may be the most powerful medicine on earth."[11] In our movement toward another and telling our story with integrity, our scattered lives are put back together again.

Our true self can only arrive on the scene when our story is spoken and heard.

Trusted friendships allow us the space to reflect and make sense of our story. As Daniel Goleman observes, "We don't know who we are until we hear ourselves speaking the story of our lives to those we trust."[12] Our true self can only arrive on the scene when our story is spoken and heard. Trusted friends can offer perspective and insights that might otherwise go undetected. They help us listen to our lives, offer clarity, and point our discrepancies and patterns of relating of which we may be unaware.

Every time we tell our story,
it becomes a point of healing.

Hidden things come to light but not in a neurotic shame-inducing way. Once noticed, we can offer those things to God for grace to do its work. We assemble these new truths in our stories. We begin to see something different of ourselves, of our wounds, and of God. We begin to experience our story in the realities of forgiveness, restoration, and hope. Every time we tell our story, it becomes a point of healing. We begin to find meaning and witness the emergence of our true selves. The secrecy of shame loses its grip as we tell our story over and over until a new story surfaces. We begin to see our smaller story as part of God's greater story of redemption.

For good or for bad, remembering our stories defines us and reminds us who we are. That's why our kids love looking at pictures of their growing up years and love hear the story behind the pictures. The pictures remind them where they came from and who they are. As Keith Anderson insightfully notes, "We live in the stories we remember most."[13] That's why God instituted the Passover as a way of reminding the Hebrew people over and over of the covenant-keeping God who led them out of slavery. Passover reminds them of their identity as God's chosen people. Similarly, Communion is an embodied, communal, and repeated act of remembering. We remember not only what Jesus did on the Cross but who we are in Christ and what that means for us today.

As we begin to rehearse and live
into a different story
it becomes the new master narrative
of our lives.

As trusted friends help us assemble new stories of grace into our lives, we create a different story to be told over and over. As we begin to rehearse and live into a different story it becomes the new master narrative of our lives.

Practicing Confession: Being Made Joyfully Whole

James 5:16 instructs, "Make this your common practice: Confess your sins to each other and pray for each other so that you can live together whole and healed." The Greek word for confess means "to profess openly and joyfully."[14] I am unsure whether I have ever considered confession as merry, but it must have something to do with the result of our confession. The Greek word for *sin* means "to miss or wander from the path of uprightness and honour, to do wrong or go wrong."[15]

Sin reveals why we do what we do. Our inner struggle produces the 'stuff' that appears at times in our lives.

Jesus is present in our most honest, most difficult places.

My unauthorized interpretation of confession entails the following: "As honestly and unguarded as we can, as often as we can, admit to each other all the ways we have lived untruthfully to ourselves and each other, so our disintegrated lives might be made joyfully whole." Confession—telling our story—creates a space where our souls are healed. Confession is not just for the 'big' stuff; confession lives most robustly in our daily conversations with trusted friends. Like the men on the Road to Emmaus, Jesus shows up amid weariness and disappointment in honest conversation and vulnerability. Jesus is present in our most honest, most difficult places.

Listen to Your Life in Solitude

The more I practice solitude, the more I begin to see solitude differently. The noise of our world has a way of separating us not only from God but from ourselves. More than a place to connect with God, solitude also becomes a space of self-reflection where we better acquaint ourselves with who we are. In other words, when we make a place for solitude and silence, we make room for ourselves.

Recently I taught a class on "Hearing the Voice of God." Those who attended listened carefully and engaged thoughtfully in the discussion. One gal hesitantly raised her hand and quietly asked, "What if I am afraid of what I might hear?" Surprisingly, many others nodded in agreement. Hearing God speak to us can be a scary thing. We are painfully aware of our failures and shortcomings and deeply afraid of hearing the words, "You are not enough."

Consider how one leader described her hidden life:

> I could use several words to describe how I feel about my relationship with the Lord. (Relationship? What relationship??) I feel like a failure, a fraud, undisciplined, weak, guilty, and most of all, desperate. I feel empty, used up, and don't know how to get filled up again. And I wonder if it will always be like this. The fear of God's condemning voice keeps me from listening or lingering. (Goodness knows, I bully and berate myself enough with "shoulds" and "oughts."

Each of us are familiar with our inner critic that tells us we are unworthy. In solitude, however, we hear, deep in our hearts, the voice of the One who calls us Beloved. We don't hear condemnation (Rom 8:1). We only hear an invitation. I have never forgotten this quote by Brennan Manning I read some years ago, which has profoundly forged my identity as the Beloved of God: "Being the beloved is our identity, the core of our existence. It is not merely a lofty thought, an inspiring idea, or a name among many names. It is the name by which God knows us and the way He relates to us."[16]

I am no longer defined by my brokenness, although much of me still needs healing.

Our identity as the beloved of God forms when we hear God's voice speak this to us personally. In the place of quiet with God, I hear these life-giving words spoken to me over and over. As I allow this deep-seated truth to saturate my heart, it quietly becomes real. I am no longer defined by my brokenness, although much of me still needs healing. No longer do my failures and regrets command center stage. If you ask me who I am, I will answer that my belovedness is the most truthful thing about me. My belovedness is my most essential identity.

Our greatest safety of self-discovery lies in our union with Jesus. The only way we become willingly and ruthlessly honest with ourselves and what is going on in our lives is when we begin to notice and accept God's unflinching, relentless love. Slowly, surely, we discover this new familiarity, comfort, and longing of feeling at home.

Listen to Your Life with Self-Compassion

Self-knowledge is important, but just as essential to wholeheartedness is learning to love ourselves regardless of what self-examination brings to light. Maybe you are a bit of a self-kindness skeptic. In this age of narcissism, shouldn't we be focused instead on self-denial, you ask? Or better yet, self-forgetfulness? Well, yes, but the road to self-denial is an indirect one. It first passes by way of God's acceptance. And, yes, we do well to deny ourselves destructive outward vices—so long as we also deny destructive inward patterns of self-condemnation and self-criticism. Both kinds of self-denial become easier when we know we're loved by God and free to make mistakes.

Self-knowledge is important,
but even more essential to wholeheartedness
is learning to love ourselves
regardless of what self-examination
brings to light.

Self-empathy entails stopping and noticing with curiosity and compassion, without judging, what is going on in your life. It means that instead of self-condemnation, you give yourself permission to not be perfect, to fail, and to simply be human. Lean into the process of becoming, instead of needing to have 'arrived.' As Brown notes, "I now see how owning our story and loving ourselves through that process is the bravest thing we will ever do."[17]

Be as kind to yourself as you are to others.

Too often we ignore our anxiety and the intensity of ministry. We disregard our needs and push through. We don't pay attention to the impact of our work. Left unchecked, these things breed even more exhaustion, fear, and feelings of being overwhelmed. Self-empathy prioritizes our wellness when self-care has been ignored. Self-empathy includes remembering that hidden in our failures are good things, like courage. Permit yourself to try new things and fail. Lean into the discomfort. Be as kind to yourself as you are to others.

Listen to Your Life in Lament

The intensity and frantic pace of ministry life rarely allow the time needed for leaders to grieve the losses, hurts, and wounds. According to some scholars, over forty percent of the Psalms are prayers of lament.[18] Typically, we are unfamiliar and/or uncomfortable with the laments of others or ourselves. If someone displays sadness, we quickly jump in with a Scripture to try to coax them to a place other than their pain. Often, we are trying to placate our discomfort. We are afraid that they (and maybe ourselves) may never recover from that dark place. The Psalms demonstrate that lament helps us to recover a sense of God's presence. The Psalmists (no matter how bleak the circumstances) almost always end their psalms with a shout of praise to God and the assurance of His help that is sure to come.

Scripture reveals that Jesus is near and available to the brokenhearted. However, when we try to run from, deny, or cover our pain, we often short-circuit the process that lament offers—the process that makes us human. When we boldly hold our sorrows, fears, and anger in God's presence—when we speak truth from our depth, God meets us there.

Keith Anderson writes, "Spirituality does not stop when we grieve. Biblical spirituality is not a spirituality of denial of loss, pain, grief, and depth; it is a spirituality that calls us to continued attention even in the midst of our pain."[19] Deep calls to deep; this allows what is deep is in us to connect to what's in the depths of God. Our spirit connects with the Holy Spirit through lament. This is profound because it is coming from a deep place. Our cries sound so unfiltered and messy, and this is what makes lament powerful. The prayer of lament proves difficult, but it could serve as our deepest and truest prayer. The moment we begin to bring these things out in the open into God's presence the possibility of resurrection arises.

The moment we begin to bring
these things out in the open
into God's presence
the possibility of resurrection arises.

A friend lost his daughter several years ago in a car accident. He said that the only thing he could pray for six months was Psalm 88, a Psalm of Lament. Instead of 'bucking up' or soldiering on, he allowed lament to give voice and words to the ache and devastation of his soul. Only after he could be with what was real could he move on and find healing. The point is to turn to God in whatever state we are in. That's why we can pray even when we don't feel like it. Prayer can be as a sigh deep in our spirit. The sighs of the Spirit are heard most clearly in the laments of the Psalms.

What do you need to lament? What do you need to grieve or sorrow over? Much of what needs lamenting comes through loss: loss of a loved one; a job, a dream, a relationship, physical health, and more. Find a quiet place and allow yourself to embrace your loss in the presence of God.

Recovering Our Calling and Identity

In 2010, the movie, "Alice in Wonderland," starring Jonny Depp as the Mad Hatter, came out in theaters. My husband and I went to see it. Walking out of the movie theater, I grabbed my husband's arm and blurted, "Did you catch it?" He looked a little dazed, like I was asking a trick question. Alice returns to Wonderland through the rabbit hole. Everyone in Wonderland knew that someday Alice would return to fulfill her identity and calling to free the people of Wonderland by from the power of the evil Queen of Hearts. Everyone is excited to see Alice again! Everyone except Alice. She forgot about her first trip to Wonderland and her promise to return. She forgot about her destiny of killing the Evil Queen to free the creatures of Wonderland. The Mad Hatter confronts her: "You don't slay. You've lost your muchness." Pointing to her heart he said, "In there … something is missing." The Mad Hatter revealed that Alice's destiny was deeply tied to her very being.

Since that day, a prayer I pray often is, "Lord, help me not to lose my muchness."

The Mad Hatter revealed that Alice's destiny was deeply tied to her very being.

Re-Membering Your Story

Sometimes we forget who we are and what we are called to do. Telling and retelling our story, is a way of re-membering; a way of bringing our scattered lives back together. In 1 Samuel 25 David, the would-be king of Israel needs a re-membering of who he is and what he has been called to do.

Not at his own initiative but God's, David has been chosen from the grassy fields of a shepherd and anointed as king by the prophet Samuel. However, he has not yet been given the kingdom. David has an amazing awareness of God's active presence guiding the events of his life, trusting that God can bring about His purposes. How do we know this? When given the opportunity to kill Saul, David shows restraint, much to the chagrin of his fighting men (1 Sam 24). David is not about manipulating God's story to suit his own purposes or how he thinks this plan should unfold. David trusts God's initiative, timing, and his ability to bring his purposes to secure David's throne. David knows he is participating in something greater than himself, and he is unwilling to take the kingdom by force. But somewhere along the way, David loses sight of this reality.

David is now on the run. King Saul is chasing David with murderous intent. He is hiding with his band of men in the wilderness. They come upon an expansive place where a man named Nabal pastured his 3,000 sheep. Without taking anything for themselves, they protect Nabal's sheep and herdsmen during a time of shearing. Shearing is a time of celebration for the bountiful provision it will bring.

As strangers who safeguard Nabal's business from marauders, David sends his servants to warmly greet Nabal. He makes a reasonable request: a donation of food for himself and his men. The passage notes, however, that Nabal was a Calebite, a less-than-savory distinction. "He was surly and mean in his dealings" (1 Sam 25:3). So, when Nabal receives David's request, Nabal mocks David. "Who is this David?" At first, we think Nabal knows who David is—the anointed next King of Israel. His second question betrays him: "Who is this son of Jesse?" Nabal shows he knows David, though he speaks of him with contempt.

Nabal refuses David's reasonable request for hospitality. In fact, he insults (shames) David as being with the riffraff of wilderness outlaws. Nabal's name means "fool," the Bible's most contemptuous term (Ps 14:1). The Hebrew word from which "fool" is derived means "to collapse." With no awareness of God and His activity in the world, Nabal's world eventually collapses (1 Sam 25:38).

Nabal might have given a civil answer and made the denial, as modest as the request was, but instead his narrow soul speaks indignantly of David as an insignificant man unworthy of his generosity. David, usually so full of God, is now full of himself (1 Sam 25:21-22). The scene drastically takes a turn for the worst. David had just shown great restraint and tenderness with murderous King Saul because he could see him as the Lord's anointed. However, he cannot see Nabal for the fool he is. Blinded by shame, David loses sight of his destiny and God's divine activity in his life.

Blinded by shame, David loses sight of his destiny and God's divine activity in his life.

David gathers 400 men, instructing them to strap on their swords. He is going to wipe out Nabal and his entire male household. Puffed up with resentment and rehearsing the destruction of Nabal, David threatens to throw away his kingdom in one shame-induced loss of perspective.

When Nabal's wife, Abigail, hears of David's outrage and his plan of action, she intercedes. In contrast to Nabal (the fool), the name Abigail means "her Father's joy." She meets David upon the march. In a poetic plea, Abigail reminds David of his destiny and God's ability to bring it about:

> Please forgive your servant's presumption. The Lord your God will certainly make a lasting dynasty for my lord, because you fight the Lord's battles, and no wrongdoing will be found in you as long as you live. Even though someone is pursuing you to take your life,

> the life of my lord will be bound securely in the bundle of the living by the Lord your God, [emphasis added] but the lives of your enemies he will hurl away as from the pocket of a sling. When the Lord has fulfilled for my lord every good thing he promised concerning him and has appointed him ruler over Israel, my lord will not have on his conscience the staggering burden of needless bloodshed or of having avenged himself. And when the Lord your God has brought my lord success, remember your servant (1 Sam 25:28-31).

Abigail reminds David of the faithful, promise-keeping activity of God in his life. God himself, she assures, orchestrates his days and will bring about the kingdom for which he has been anointed and appointed. Even in this moment, God is keeping David, through Abigail's intervention. She is participating with God to keep David securely in Jehovah's personal care and protection.

Abigail reminds David of the faithful, promise-keeping activity of God in his life.

When David loses sight of God, Abigail reminds David of his God-honoring life, his true self, and divine destiny. Abigail reminds David of his story as part of God's redemptive story. David recovers from his shame and finds his footing again.

This could be your story as well. Don't let the foolishness of others cause you to forget your calling and destiny. God is dynamically at work orchestrating your days! He is fulfilling His every good purpose through you. Don't get derailed in ministry or allow shame to rule the day. You are part of God's redemptive story. Find your footing again!

Throughout this book we have examined and unpacked Jesus's instructions in Mark 12:29-30, to love oneself and others—the essential dimensions of human integration and foundation for spiritual leadership. In the Introduction, we learned that love is, by nature, focused attention, i.e., showing up all the way and being 'all there.' Thus, in order to love, we need to train ourselves to be fully present. Thus, Jesus was inviting us to train ourselves to be *fully present* to these three things that matter most, with priority on loving God.

In chapter 6 we considered how being present to God was a way of cultivating intimacy with Him in such a way that the life of Christ is released in us. Chapters 7 and 8 offered us the practices that cultivate a way of being with God

Chapters 9 and 10 examined the emotional/hidden life of the leader and the practices needed to be present to self.

Now in chapters 11 and 12 we conclude with the third dimension of holistic living and leading: being fully present to others.

11

Present to Others

"To be 'on mission' is to cultivate the life of Christ in us that we might embody the love and character of Christ to the world." —Gail Johnsen

A Way of Moving in the World

I have consistently emphasized that the Spirit's work of integration is never just about us. Giving our attention and being fully present to God is not just so we can live with a lasting sense of His presence. Giving our full attention to the complexities of our inner being is not just so we can experience freedom from self-condemnation or shame. The word *attention* comes from the Latin *attendere*, meaning "to reach toward." Rather than faith being a private affair, our faith takes on a participatory and cultural reality. In other words, our formation has to make a difference in the way we live toward others.

Rather than faith being a private affair, our faith takes on a participatory and cultural reality.

Perhaps the most practical expressions of a truly integrated spiritual maturity may be how we reflect Jesus in acts of genuine compassion, kindness, and hospitality (Matt 25:40). The Church is called to embody the truth expressed in love, compassion, and mercy to others. Jesus said these things should characterize kingdom people and God's redemptive mission in the world—not a cause or a program but a way of moving and relating in the world. To share the gospel is not to propagate an idea, a plan, or a vision. The gospel is us! The good news incarnated and proclaimed through the reality of Christ's presence in us to a hurting world.

Something is Wrong

When my husband and I were in the first semester of our freshman year of Bible school, we took a required course on evangelism. The class was based on a book that was considered *the* text on evangelism at that time. The book popularized witnessing as a systematic strategy with clearly defined methods and design. The basis of engagement centered around two qualifying questions that proved a person's need to be saved. The ultimate goal in this strategy was conversion.

After twelve weeks of training and equipping, our final assignment was to go the University of Washington campus and use our newly acquired skills and lead someone to Jesus. I walked on campus that day with the premise that it was up to me to convert someone. Armed with a clever presentation of the gospel, a preprogrammed plan of action, and a solid argument of my faith, my job that day was to convict, confront, and convince someone of his or her theological errors and him or her them believe and behave as I do.

"Um, excuse me, if you were to die tonight do you know…" "Oh, okay. I will get lost."

Not only did I not lead anyone to the Lord, but by the standards we were taught, we were a dismal failure. More often than not, this way of evangelism took a top-down approach. It emulated an air of superiority, control, and manipulation. Sharing the Good News became more about how I could impress others with my elaborate knowledge of the Bible or mount a good defense if anyone questioned my faith. Much too often this approach became an "us versus them" and "I am right, you are wrong" approach, too. It became about the haves and the have nots—those who were 'in' and those who were 'not.' The 'nots' were seen as a threat to be discredited at all costs.

This approach turned us into mean people. If you don't think so, try disagreeing with someone's belief preference. I am not talking about negating false doctrine. Sound doctrine is essential in matters of faith, but even so, we must exhibit grace to those who disagree with us.

I have been on the receiving end of someone's threatened belief system, and it has been neither kind nor pleasant. Being well taught does not make us more loving. Without pulling any punches, Brennan Manning writes, "The idolatry of ideas has left me puffed up, narrowminded, and intolerant of any idea that does not coincide with mine."[1] Tragically, so many years ago, our faith had become a belief system to defend at all costs. Yet, our superior posture rarely changes anyone's life.

Yet, our superior posture
rarely changes anyone's life.

Most troubling is that people became our 'projects.' If someone made a decision for Christ, we etched a notch on our evangelism belt and walked away self-satisfied that we 'got another one into the kingdom.' This released us from any further personal expectation, relational engagement, or ongoing discipleship. The goal of our evangelism was always about an end result. We were thankful to be off the hook when it came to engaging real, hurting people.

There is something wrong when we care more about being right than how we treat other people. For too long our lives have not convincingly demonstrated the reality of our message. Our hypocrisy did not go unnoticed. Rather than a message of love, the Church preached a message of judgmentalism that ignored the heart of the gospel for ourselves. The perceived onramp to evangelical Christianity was an imposed compliance to a list of dos and don'ts, institutional attendance, or consent to certain beliefs.

There is something wrong
when we care more about being right
than how we treat other people.

We have to find a better way.

Pirate Radio

The British station, Radio Caroline, was founded in 1964 by Ronan O'Rahilly, an Irish musician manager and businessman. Radio Caroline began initially to circumvent the record companies' control of popular music broadcasting in the kingdom and the BBC's radio broadcasting. At the time, regulations determined what could be played during work hours and promoted music styles that would generate a more focused worker—music someone could whistle along to but that wouldn't be distracting.

The more progressive pop chart music was given a couple of hours on Sunday evenings. Commercial radio wasn't yet an option. The guardians of the publicly owned BBC considered pop music immoral, antisocial, and unfit for public broadcast.

The founder of Radio Caroline named it after seeing a picture of young Caroline Kennedy crawling around under the desk of her dad while he was on an important business call. To him it represented a playful disruption of authority. On March 28, (Easter Sunday) 1964, Radio Caroline was born in a converted 702-ton former Danish passenger ferry. The ship was converted into a broadcasting station offshore without knowing who, if anyone, would be listening. Their first song: "It's All Over Now" by the Rolling Stones turned out to be prescient. By 1967, there was an explosion of popularity. Caroline was claiming half of the listeners in the UK. A lot of upcoming bands—the Beatles, the Who—can thank Pirate Radio for part of their success at home and abroad.

He came to give us and those outside
a religious system entrance into
the kingdom of God.

Pirates can show up anywhere a system becomes rigid making it hard or even impossible for newcomers to succeed. Pirates protest against a blocked world. We have made Christianity about so many things: right doctrine, right behavior, right belief, right methods, rules, regulations, and laws. In doing so, we have blocked access to the reality of Christ. Jesus came into a religious system that made it hard for newcomers to get in. He arrived as a disruption of authority. He came to give us and those outside a religious system entrance into the kingdom of God.

Encounters with Spiders

A few years ago, after a morning service, we met a young woman in our lobby.

"How did you happen to come today?" I inquired.

"I was at a gas station this morning, and I asked someone pumping gas if there was a church nearby. They offered me a ride here." (Yay, them!) She had tattoos and piercing in all the visible places, dreadlocks down to the middle of her back, and ragged layers of clothing. Dirt and grease were crusted under her fingernails, and she certainly didn't smell like me. She also had a pit bull by her side.

We introduced ourselves, and I asked her name.

"My rail name is Spider."

"That's an interesting name! Would you tell me about it?"

Spider told us she had been riding the railroad cars (underneath and illegally) for almost three years. We learned about a subculture of rail riders and the difference between a hobo and a vagabond. (Spider insisted she was *not* a hobo.)

We also found out that she was raised in a Baptist preacher's home in Texas. She spoke lovingly of her daddy and knew he missed her, but she had not called home in quite a while. I asked her what kept her from going home. She said she was on a journey that she needed to take right now. She spoke with an understanding of grace. She was kind, articulate, and respectful. I think we could have been longtime friends.

"How can we help you?" I asked.

"I need to get to Portland by tomorrow. The coal car headed that direction doesn't leave the station until Tuesday," she responded. (The rail riders know all the traffic patterns of the trains.)

"How about we buy you a ticket so you can ride inside the boxcar?" I suggested.

With a little encouragement, we convinced her to do so. We loaded Spider and her dog and drove to our home. I ran inside and poured almonds into a gallon zip-lock bag, (for protein) and bagged up some dog food. We asked about her favorite fast-food restaurant, and she responded, "Arby's." We grabbed her two sandwiches and headed for the train station.

My husband approached the ticket counter, but when the cashier saw Spider's dog, she refused to allow her to board. No amount of persuasion worked.

"It's okay," assured Spider. "Just take me to the highway, and I can hitchhike to Portland." When Spider noticed our hesitancy, she assured us she had done this many times before.

"Have you ever had a bad pick up?" I asked.

"Just once," she replied, looking down.

We started down the interstate highway, and Spider instructed us to take the first on/off ramp to drop her off.

"People haven't yet got to full speed on the on-ramp, and they are more willing to pull over," she explained. She'd done this a time or two.

If evangelism is anything, it is opening our eyes to God's grace (activity) in others' lives.

We prayed with her before we got out of the car with her. I reached into my wallet and gave her everything I had. As I placed the bills in her hand, I looked in her eyes and said, "Your daddy loves you very much. Promise me you will call him."

"I will," she promised.

We left Spider on the side of that interstate on-ramp and pulled away with tears in our eyes. There was no dramatic, "come to Jesus" moment. My husband and I simply entered her story and played our part in her journey of God's redemptive grace. Too often we hold a mental framework that witnessing 'success' is shaped by powerful actions and climactic endings. We often miss the smallness of the kingdom found in every grace-filled story. Everyone has a grace-filled story to be told, but we only hear it if we enter his or her story and listen. Every conversation matters. Every act of kindness does matter. If evangelism is anything, it is opening our eyes to God's grace (activity) in others' lives. This approach will become essential as we consider our new cultural realties.

Changing Cultural Narratives

We now live in a post-Christendom context with undeniable different cultural narratives than the modern era. Previously, we had a system that assumed the existence of a personal God. We had a faith grounded in religious participation and particular beliefs, but those assumptions have changed. Coming to the end of the modern era, we are now entrenched in a new wave of culture, a secular post-Christian age.

Typically, when we visit other countries and cultures, to make ourselves understood to the people from these different linguistic and cultural backgrounds, we must make the effort to learn their languages and ways of thinking. We must approach them as they are, not how we wish they were. We must do the same to those in this new prevailing culture.

I do not intend to present an exhaustive treatise on our post-Christian/secular culture. There are many helpful and reliable resources available for a more comprehensive understanding. However, I hope to merely emphasize that a radically changing culture requires a different missional approach. Digging our heels in, lamenting change, or doubling down our efforts will not serve this generation. We dare not write off people who think differently than we do. They are the ones we are called to love. The message of the gospel remains the same, but we will have to reconsider the most effective way to communicate its truth on their terms.

We need apologetics, but not any apologetic will do. Rather than focusing on formulaic presentations, we must understand that context is essential. We are reaching people who have been born into a particular time, place, and cultural narrative. They have inherited a complex story. Their assumptions have profoundly shaped their behavior and thinking.

To truly understand someone's unbelief, we must go beneath the surface and identify these powerful and pervasive assumptions. One such inherited assumption presumes that transcendence, that is, God and His activity in the world, doesn't exist or have any effect on you. Root explains, "The meaning that's been washed away (or at least radically eroded) is a clear vision of divine action, the sure sense that God indeed causes things in our world and directs our lives."[2] Belief in God is considered simply an ideology and just one of many beliefs and lifestyle options available to choose from. Thus, religious pluralism emerges, declaring that all religious systems are equally true; none are superior or "truer" than another.

The assumption also exists that there is no absolute truth; only one's interpretation of truth matters. This means truth is relative to each person, and certainty of knowledge is an impossibility. In such a cultural climate, any claims of absolute truth are seen as exclusive and intolerant. Embracing a heightened expressive individualism, one's experience, not biblical truth, often serves as the primary arbiter of truth.

In other words, we make our own truth. According to Barna research, truth is increasingly regarded as something felt, or relative (44 percent), rather than something known, or absolute (35 percent).[3] Thus, any claims to universal or absolute truths, morals, or values are also rejected.

Christianity, therefore, by our current cultural assessment, does not have the right to claim it has the truth. Root explains, "God is no longer personal nor is there any expectation that God might break into our lives at any moment. To argue for faith is to simply argue for an ideology."[4] With God removed from the fabric of human experience, this logically gives rise to the belief that the only thing that exists is the material world. Our existence is a 'closed' system in that there is nothing outside of what we see. There is no ultimate, transcendent design or Creator.

Similarly, people reject metanarratives, an all-encompassing worldview or belief system, such as God's redemptive story. The central belief is that there is no grand story. Nothing hangs everything together. All we have are smaller stories without rhyme, or reason, or author.

Added to these radical cultural changes, we are met with a constantly distracted culture that keeps people shielded from deep reflection, challenging questions, or considering complex, personal implications. With frantic and fatigued minds, people's cognitive attention is dispersed, and they are ill-prepared to wrestle with knotty conversations about God or hold compelling tensions. Technology, also, asks too little of us and has robbed people of the ability to be present, patient, creative, and/or committed.

How do we bring a message of Jesus to a culture so deeply skeptical about truth claims, rejects a greater Story, believes that any religion will lead them to God, and struggles with complex realities? This is new culture in which we are called to lead. How can we be fully present to others in this new context in a way that matters?

A Posture of Listening

As I write, our nation is reeling from the tragic death of George Floyd, a black American, killed by white police officers in Minneapolis. Floyd's death brought a tipping point in our nation against the eradication of a centuries-old systemic and structural racism for a people who have been silenced, brutalized, and minimized. Cries called for sweeping police reform, racial equality, and an end to deeply rooted racial discrimination. Equally, cries went out for reconciliation, solidarity, and a posture of honest, genuine, and gracious listening and understanding from both sides.

In the wake of this racial unrest, the president of Northwest University, Joe Castleberry, in a blog tilted, "Leading by Ear," notes,

> The occasion offers an opportunity to listen deeply. Leadership requires listening patiently to people, suspending the argument one wants to make in order to hear carefully another person's perspective. Allowing speech with the impatient and clearly indicated intention to ignore what the other has said and get your point

> across both irritates and alienates. Truly listening creates the open space where people can meet in dialogue. Some on every side will change their minds through dialogue.[5]

Attentive listening may be
the most significant relational skill
a ministry leader can possess today.

Attentive listening may be the most significant relational skill a ministry leader can possess today. In an intensely practical way, an appealing invitation to relationship to non-Christians comes through an attentive/listening ('all there') posture of another. Through attentive listening, we don't impose our beliefs on them. Rather, we play off of cultural curiosity and constructive conversations. In 1 Corinthians 9:19-23 (MSG), the Apostle Paul writes,

> Even though I am free of the demands and expectations of everyone, I have voluntarily become a servant to any and all in order to reach a wide range of people: religious, nonreligious, meticulous moralists, loose-living immoralists, the defeated, the demoralized—whoever. *I didn't take on their way of life. I kept my bearings in Christ—but I entered their world and tried to experience things from their point of view* [emphasis added]. I've become just about every sort of servant there is in my attempts to lead those I meet into a God-saved life. I did all this because of the Message. I didn't just want to talk about it; I wanted to be in on it!

Paul makes it clear that he did not get pulled into the differing cultural surrounding or leave his faith behind. He remained steadfast and fixated in his missional purpose. However, making spacious room for those outside of faith, Paul willingly and intentionally entered their world to view the world from their perspective. His humility became a way of leading others, that they might eventually embrace the gospel story. This not in any way to say the Church should dumb-down its theology or doctrines but by coming alongside others, as Joshua Chatraw, notes, "not with a posture of opposition, but rather with a posture of invitation: 'Come, taste, and see.'"[6]

Making spacious room for those outside of faith, Paul willingly and intentionally entered their world to view the world from their perspective.

So how do we proclaim the gospel to a world that thinks differently than we do? A very simple answer to a very complex question is, "Listen." Ask for a person's story. Welcome dialogue. Stop defending your position. Listen without judgment. Listening implies inviting them into relationship. Listening, first and foremost, is about attentiveness: being fully present in the moment, focused, and responsive to the one who is speaking.

When Jesus gave us the command to love others, He placed a listening posture, a way of being present, as the bedrock of being a loving person.

Love has often been defined as a choice. We have also heard love defined as a verb, something we do. These are both true. However, you will not choose to love or choose to act lovingly if, first, the object of your love has not captured your attention. Belden Lane observes, "One can only love what one stops to observe."[7] Thus, we won't put someone's needs above our own or intentionally prefer another until we have first noticed them and listened to them.

When Jesus gave us the command to love others, He placed a listening posture, a way of being present, as the bedrock of being a loving person. In other words, giving our full attention to others comes through a posture of listening and embodies the very act of love itself. Perhaps the most important walking expression of Jesus in our distracted and disconnected world is listening. As Michael Frost notes, "The church must adopt a posture of active listening, of attentiveness to the disenchantment of our neighbors, in order to know how to offer something more than the deathly, heartless, hedonistic world of secularism."[8] Rather than seeing our culture as an adversary to be dealt with or ignored, we must understand that God is actively on mission Himself. He is inviting us to be in on it simply through sincere friendships where love is our only agenda.

Thus, our love for Christ is best expressed in the hard work of loving our neighbor. What if our neighbors come to know us by our love and not the strength of our arguments? What if our faith is not a static belief we tenaciously cling to, but a way of living and moving gracefully in the world?

Thus, our love for Christ is best expressed in the hard work of loving our neighbor.

What if the quality of our love became the basis of the reality of the gospel? Instead of being right, what if sharing the gospel includes a willingness to remain fully and personally present, without judging, or the need to fix or 'save' another person. This would mean allowing each person to be seen, heard, and valued just as they are. When people know they are loved, all sorts of possibilities open up.

12

Listening: The First Act of Love

"Being heard is so close to being loved that for the average person
they are almost indistinguishable."[1]

Every Tat has a Story

I have been surprised over the last several years of how wrong I've been on so many things. I was sure I had all the right answers and that my theology was superior to everyone else's. I spent too many years defending a belief system which, in effect, shut down conversation, learning, and growing—mostly my own.

In 2019, after a Sunday morning service, we went to lunch at our local Applebee's restaurant with some friends. The cute, twenty-something waitress was kind and attentive. She wore a black knit sleeve covering the length of one of her arms. Apparently, Applebee's requires that their staff's tattoos be covered. Noticing the sleeve, a man in our party commented to her, "What's a pretty girl like you doing covered in tattoos?" She responded cordially, "Because they make me even prettier."

What if my friend instead had entered her world? What if he said, "Tell me about your tats!" Every tat has a story. We have to allow others to have their own thoughts, feel their own feelings, and believe their own beliefs without attacking them or running their words through our critical filers. Who does not want to be known, valued, and delighted in as they are? This may mean becoming comfortable with dangling or unresolved conversations. Some of the most authentic conversations are the ones ongoing.

Becoming comfortable with someone's story so different than our own is difficult. It requires surrendering our need to be right. It requires patience, curiosity, asking perceptive and open-ended questions, and taking seriously the life-giving power that listening offers to others. As we relax and take our agenda off the table, we can pay attention, listen to God, and see where He is working. Instead of fixating on fixing, we listen for the 'story behind the story.' Adam McHugh agrees, "Good listening starts with the scandalous premise that this conversation is not about you."[2] As I said before, everyone has a grace-filled story to be told if only we will enter their story and listen.

As we relax and take our agenda off the table,
we can pay attention, listen to God,
and see where He is working.

Years ago, a friend in our church had a non-Christian friend who was dying of cancer. A group of our ladies rallied around this woman. We prayed and prayed over her, organized meals, and invited her to our women's Bible study. Truthfully, our intent was to lead her to Jesus before she died. After praying intensely for her yet another time, she blurted out, "Are you concerned about my soul or about me?" Ouch ... Loving others as has to be more than just getting them to say the sinner's prayer. Parker Palmer concurs. "Here's the deal," he says. "The human soul doesn't want to be advised or fixed or saved. It simply wants to be witnessed—to be seen, heard and companioned exactly as it is."[3] Too often we treat people as projects to be recruited, reached, or proselytized, and in doing so we dehumanize them. It put us in a 'top-down' position with an agenda rather than relating in a shared brokenness of humanity.

Too often we treat people as projects to be recruited, reached, or proselytized, and in doing so we dehumanize them.

Instead of requiring immediate conversion as the litmus of our witness, listening to and loving others where they are allows kindness and grace to begin their work of transformation. In undramatic ways, we get to play a part of someone's journey. Perhaps, then, somewhere along the way, without them even knowing it, they fall in love with Jesus simply because we loved them as Jesus does. Instead of worrying if we are saying the right things, what if apologetics is more about how we love than what we say?

Hospitable Listening

A few years ago, a young woman who I didn't know well approached me and asked, "Can we go for coffee?" I knew that her asking wasn't just to get to know me better; she needed someone to talk to. Almost every week I have the privilege of sitting at this table. Each person comes with his or her own story of brokenness. Brokenness appears a thousand different ways. However, I never consider it my job to fix, solve, or make others happy. I am not that smart, and most often they aren't there to be fixed. They simply want to be heard. I offer them a safe place to share their stories.

My friend shared her story of bad decisions, doubts, and confusion. She assumed God was disappointed in her and wondered if she had been disqualified from God's grace. One misconception of the spiritual life is that God only comes to us when we get our 'stuff' together. Sometimes people want me to help them get it together so God will do this or that for them.

However, instead of rescuing, I listened. As I listened, I noticed how God was actively at work right in that moment, in small ways, in the middle of her 'untogetherness.' I was there to help her discover for herself God's grace embedded in her brokenness.

Nestled in every difficult circumstance is an invitation to wholeness. Yet, too often in the rush and weight of our days, we can miss the ways God makes himself and His ways known. That's where I come in. As a leader, I am charged with helping people stay alive to God. "Pay attention," I whisper to her. "This can lead to someplace good."

Being fully present to the world
must include an incarnational
way of relating to people.

What if one of our most essential roles as leaders included leading others to recognize their own stories of grace? What if our greatest privilege was to walk with them and watch God's work in them unfold? Romans 2:4 tells us, "It is kindness that leads to repentance." Being fully present to the world must include an incarnational way of relating to people. We offer open-hearted, welcoming, and grace-filled presence to others. In an intensely practical way, our curious, non-judgmental, and hospitable posture is an appealing invitation into relationships with non-Christians. As Dutch priest, Henri Nouwen, explains,

"Listening offers others freedom from judgment, creating space for transformation to take place."[4]

The Gift of Presence

In our secular age, experience equals reality. Thus, only when something has upended one's life can faith often be discussed at all. Loss and brokenness may become the place where room for the possibility of a transcendent God may open up. To the grieving and broken, we offer the gift of presence. We are with them in and through their pain. As we give them room to examine the arc of their lives, they may perhaps notice the God already revealing himself to them. Our job is not to prove that God is actively present but to help people to be curious and open to the possibility and look around for the transcendent.

Loss and brokenness may
become the place where
room for the possibility
of a transcendent God
may open up.

We desire that people experience faith in our evolving culture. This must include our willingness to walk with them through the redemptive landscape that the work grace is already emerging in their lives. Entering into their lives, the active, living, functioning presence of Christ that flows into us is at their disposal. We show up, we watch, we pray, we wait, we stay, not willing for them to be alone.

Part of the ministry leader's role in a postmodern/secular age is that of a spiritual director. We help others be attentive to grace by remaining part of the events of their lives and looking together for God's presence and movements. One vital task of our witness is to validate their story. We draw them into God's greater story through our own lives. This means we must also be attentive and discerning of God's voice and action in our lives to give meaning to our words.

We help others be attentive to grace
by remaining part of the events of
their lives and looking together
for God's presence
and movements.

Our story of faith matters, especially in a secular culture that values experience. We not only listen, but in a conversational back and forth manner, we take opportunities to speak. We speak with humility; we speak to build others up and not tear down; we speak respectfully with words of grace (Eph 4:29). We return a harsh word with a soft answer (Prov 15:1). We speak truthfully of hope in our losses, help in our struggles, and a God who is real and has graciously entered into our story. As Root explains, "Maybe one of the reasons that miracles and God's speaking seems so improbable to the people in the secular age is because we never talk about them when they happen in our lives."[5]

With our lives and our mouths, we speak of the majesty and goodness of God as active and life-giving in our lives. You may be uncomfortable without a script. What if you simply remain in gracious dialogue, respecting each other's journey of faith? What if you remain attentive to opportunities to care and to speak?

Absent Presence

Attentive listening carries weighty implications in the haste of ministry. For leaders, remaining present will prove difficult. Often our minds, innocently and unwittingly, flit about, yet we may still seem physically present to the person in front of us. In a very generalized sense, leaders are poor conversationalists. To truly listen is hard. The difficulty to remain present long enough may feel like a luxury in the relentless, drivenness of our ministerial tasks.

As someone expected to have all the answers,
we often talk too much and listen very little.

As someone expected to have all the answers, we often talk too much and listen very little. The temptation to prioritizing problem-solving above listening remains ever-present. Our attention spans are short; we are busy and eager to move on. Even while the other person is speaking, we are formulating a response. We want to tell them how we handled a similar situation or offer fast advice. Sweet confronts this lack of presence: "Without laser-like focusing energy we suffer from what sociologists call 'absent presence.' Physically present we may be, but our attention drifts and pinballs, seldom in the here and now."[6] As one typically in charge, discharging information, and handing out answers, ministry leaders need intentional practices for effective listening.

Most of all, it is about showing up for others
and not being quick to answer.

There is an enormous amount of scientific and neurological research on listening skills. Almost all conclude that listening requires being fully present, which is more and more difficult as we become more and more distracted. We are not born with an active listening skillset. It is a discipline learned and honed over time. You don't need to read a book on how to listen, although reading a book on life coaching is a good place to start. I've already mentioned many of the listening skills needed. Most of all, it is about showing up for others and not being quick to answer.

A Remarkable Opportunity for the Church and Its Leaders

As we are confronted with changing cultural realities and the challenge of leading others, our ability to live authentically will become more and more essential. As Creps observes,

> There will be no substitute for a lived-out faith in the 21st century. Postmoderns expect authenticity. This is more than an issue of personal holiness. It also concerns the need to be honest and forthright. We do not have all the answers. We are weak. We do fail. A disciple maker, then, must be an authentic, flesh-and-blood person willing to expose his or her life to observation[7]

This is where a congruent life and integrated leadership become foundational. As we vulnerably and honestly share about our ongoing transformation and the wounds, struggles, setbacks, and heartaches along the way, we take our place alongside other struggling souls. At the same time, we can seamlessly share about hope beyond ourselves. We share our astonishing interaction with the relational and transcendent God.

What if our grace-filled journey,
far from complete, allows us to become
bearers of grace to a disenchanted culture?

What if our amazing journey to wholeness, lived out before others, becomes the very means that compels them toward life?

What if our grace-filled journey, far from complete, allows us to become bearers of grace to a disenchanted culture?

The message of Christ will prove most compelling when our lives reflect the reality of Christ himself as the One who is real and ever-present *with* us. When Christ echoes in our lives, we offer others an irresistible picture of Jesus.

You don't have to be an expert to sense the dramatic cultural shift. You may feel that a massive cultural chasm separates you from your neighbor with little that unites you. Engaging others who think radically different than you may feel overwhelming, intimidating, or even scary.

We are accustomed to the right answers, but no one is asking the right questions anymore. We have been comfortable having a sense of control but are now flanked by uncertainty and doubt. The temptation is to live inside our religious bubble. We may prefer to ignore or discredit the evolving culture altogether. It takes courage to leave behind the safety of our beliefs, step into someone else's unknown world, and love without expectation.

It takes courage to leave behind the safety of our beliefs, step into someone else's unknown world, and love without expectation.

Much in the process of listening, transparency, and joining God's mission is too complex for me to figure out. Perhaps you feel the same way, too. I can't predict how your conversations will play out. There is one thing, however, that is easy to understand: love your neighbor. This is Jesus's commandment, second only to loving God. Why not start there? By your example and through the words you preach, you are inviting those you serve to do the same. Teach your people to love everyone who walks through your doors. Teach them not to pause to find out if those who come are worthy or not.

Embrace the world God loves. Get close to the people for whom Jesus died. And then listen and watch—God is at work all around you, and He will be at work in and through you. This, indeed, is good news to all people.

Epilogue

Ministry is not what it used to be. In a rapidly evolving, secular culture, we will not serve our culture well by trying to do church better, doubling down our efforts, or ignoring the culture all together. The leader in the days ahead must hold out something more life-giving than an being an institutional manager, celebrity personality, or the dregs of his or her exhaustion. In the emptiness of secularism, people will yearn for something sacred, even mysterious, that can't be entirely explained. People will come to our churches, or meet us in coffee shops, to find spiritual reality and rest for their souls. (Although, they may not use those terms.) The leader of the future will need to pivot from preacher to priest, caring the souls of the weary wanderer.

This is an amazing opportunity for the Church.

May you offer others the gravity of a well-ordered soul.

May you find yourself more and more comfortable and at home in God's presence.

May you offer to others a life that is far from complete and be honest about it.

May you notice and call out the grace already at work in people's lives.

May you embrace a definition of success that comes to be defined by increasingly growing in holistic ways that ends up being for others.

May you stay open and responsive to the work of grace in you.

May you minister from a from a place of abundance rather than emptiness; rest instead of exhaustion; freedom instead of shame.

May the way you love and the way you listen allow others to be heard, valued, and ready to share their unfolding story.

May the life of Christ in you embody the love of Christ to the world.

May you model and teach this to those you lead. This is how God changes the world.

I am hopeful it will be so.

About the Author

Gail is the Pastor of Spiritual Formation at Faith Tri-Cities, Pasco, WA, where she is involved in preaching, teaching, mentoring, and leadership development. She is a popular speaker, certified life coach, and adjunct professor at Northwest University.

For over ten years Gail has led ministry leader cohorts through a nine-month spiritual formation journey. Gail is also the founder of Keeping Company with Jesus, a nine-month, online spiritual formation resource. Gail currently partners with the Northwest Ministry Network and leads The Attentive Leader retreats, a three-day retreat based on the material from *All There.*

Gail holds a Doctor of Ministry in Leadership from the Assemblies of God Theological Seminary. She has also authored *Advent Reflections: Let the Weary World Rejoice!*

Gail and her husband, Darrel, have served in full-time pastoral ministry for over forty years. They have four adult children and ten amazing grandkiddos. Gail enjoys lunch with good friends, gardening, reading, travel, and riding on the back of their Harley … because "I get to wear leathers!"

To find out more about Gail, visit her blog at gailjohnsen.com

For more information about:

THE ATTENTIVE LEADER
THREE-DAY RETREAT

Each one-day retreat (on-site or via ZOOM) covers one of the three themes of living fully present: (1) *to God,* (2) *to self,* and (3) *to others.* The retreats are strategically designed to create an environment different than a seminar. The schedule is crafted to create an informal and safe place that fosters open and honest dialogue. Participants will engage in interactive teaching, group discussions, participatory activities, and actual spiritual practices.

THE ATTENTIVE LEADER
ONE-DAY SESSION

Gail is available to speak for one all-day session.

KEEPING COMPANY WITH JESUS:
A NINE-MONTH ONLINE
SPIRITUAL FORMATION
RESOURCE

Keeping Company with Jesus is a nine-month, weekly, interactive, online resource/spiritual formation tool that begins and ends with the premise that simply being with Jesus is transformational. Weekly posts include a reading, reflection questions, and a corresponding spiritual practice. Designed to be interactive, it is best done in community and in dialogue with others. So, it's perfect for groups but can be used by individuals.

SPEAKING

Gail speaks with personal candor, passion, and humor. Her speaking engagements have included preaching in the local church (including internationally), retreats, conferences, workshops, and executive leadership teams.

LEADERSHIP COACHING

This is one-on-one leadership coaching.

TO FIND OUT MORE VISIT: GAILJOHNSEN.COM

Endnotes

Introduction

[1] C. Michael Thompson, *The Congruent Life: Following the Inward Path to Fulfilling Work and Inspired Leadership* (San Francisco: Jossey-Bass Publishers, 2000), 140.
[2] All Scripture references, unless otherwise noted, are from the New International Version.
[3] Ruth Haley Barton, *Strengthening the Soul of Your Leadership* (Downers Grove, IL: InterVarsity Press, 2008), 68.

Chapter 1

[1] Parker Palmer, *A Hidden Wholeness; The Journey Toward an Undivided Life* (San Francisco: Jossey-Bass. 2004), 7.
[2] Earl Creps, *Off-Road Disciplines: Spiritual Adventure of Missional Leaders* (San Francisco: Jossey-Bass, 2006), 131.
[3] Christopher J. H. Wright, *Mission of God: Unlocking the Bible's Grand Narrative* (Downers Grove, IL: InterVarsity Press, 2006), 62.
[4] Dallas Willard, *Renovation of the Heart: Putting on the Character of Christ* (Downers Grove, IL: InterVarsity Press, 2002), 202-203.
[5] Spoken at a lecture in September 2008, Spring Arbor University.
[6] Ruth Haley Barton, *Invitation to Silence and Solitude* (Downers Grove, IL: InterVarsity Press, 2004), 96.
[7] Patricia D. Brown, *Learning to Lead from Your Spiritual Center* (Nashville: Abingdon, 1996), 11.

Chapter 2

[1] Eugene Peterson, *The Message Study Bible* (Colorado Spring, CO: NavPress, 2012), 197.
[2] Eugene Peterson, *The Contemplative Pastor: Returning to the Art of Spiritual Direction* (Grand Rapids, MI: Eerdmans 1989), 4.
[3] Advertisement, *Discipleship Journal* issue 163 (January/February 2008): 9.

[4] Bill Gaultiere, "Reasons Why Christian Leaders Fail," Soul Shepherding Blog, accessed January 6, 2019, https://www.soulshepherding.org/reasons-christian-leaders-fail/.
[5] Ibid.
[6] Christine Valters Paintner and Lucy Wynkoop, *Lectio Divina: Contemplative Awakening and Awareness* (New York: Paulist Press, 2008), 17.
[7] Blue Letter Bible, "H1697–*dâbâr*–Strong's Hebrew Lexicon (NIV)," accessed September 9, 2017, https://www.blueletterbible.org/lang/lexicon/lexicon.cfm?Strongs=H1697&t=NIV.
[8] Leonard Sweet, *Nudge: Awakening Each Other to the God Who's Already There* (Colorado Springs, CO: David C. Cook, 2010), 145.
[9] Michael J. Quicke, "Let Him Who Has Ears, Listen," *Preaching.org Blog*, March 4, 2011, accessed January 10, 2017, http://www.preaching.org/let-him-who-has-ears-listen/.
[10] Sweet, 143.
[11] Ibid., 145.
[12] Blue Letter Bible, "G5219"—*hypakoúō*—Strong's Greek Lexicon (NIV), accessed August 31, 2020, https://www.blueletterbible.org/lang/lexicon/lexicon.cfm?t=kjv&strongs=g5219.
[13] Klyne Snodgrass, "A Hermeneutics of Hearing Informed by the Parables with Special Reference to Mark 4," *Bulletin for Biblical Research* 14 no. 1 (2004): 66-67.
[14] Joel B. Green, *Conversion in Luke-Acts* (Grand Rapids, MI: Baker Academic, 2015), 144.
[15] Klyne Snodgrass, "Between Text and Sermon: Mark 4:1-20," *Interpretation: A Journal of Bible and Theology* 67, no. 3 (July 2013): 285.
[16] See also Hebrews 3:7; 4:7.
[17] See Jeremiah 25:1-9. Four times in six verses God warns that seventy years' captivity will happen because they "did not listen."
[18] See Jeremiah 5:21; 7:24; 17:23; Isaiah 6:9-10; Ezekiel 3:7.
[19] Peterson, *Contemplative Pastor*, 4.
[20] Wright, *Mission of God*, 67.
[21] Chase Replogle, "Bonhoeffer Convinced Me to Abandon My Dream," *Christianity Today*, August 2, 2019, https://www.christianitytoday.com/pastors/2019/august-web-exclusives/bonhoeffer-convinced-me-to-abandon-my-dream.html?utm_source=leadership-html&utm_medium=Newsletter&utm_term=15728850&utm_content=

664803346&utm_campaign=email.
[22] Ibid.
[23] Ibid.

Chapter 3

[1] Joel Green, *Conversion in Luke and Acts* (Grand Rapids, MI: Baker Academic, 2015) 162.
[2] Spoken at a lecture in September 2008, Spring Arbor University.
[3] Ibid.
[4] Replogle, "Bonhoeffer Convinced Me to Abandon My Dream."
[5] John Webster quoted by Chris E. W. Green in *Surprised by God: How and Why What We Think about the Divine Matters* (Eugene, OR: Cascade Books, 2018), 67.
[6] Peterson, Contemplative Pastor, 5.
[7] Barna Research Group, "Christians on Leadership, Calling, and Career," June 3, 2013, accessed March 6, 2019, https://www.barna.com/research/christians-on-leadership-calling-and-career/.

Chapter 4

[1] Linda Stone, Linda Stone blog, accessed May 17, 2020, http://www.lindastone.net.
[2] Justin Rosenstein, quoted by Paul Lewis, "Our Minds Can Be Hijacked: The Tech Insiders Who Fear a Smartphone Dystopia," The Guardian, accessed August 31, 2020. https://www.theguardian.com/technology/2017/oct/05/smartphone-addiction-silicon-valley-dystopia#:~:text=%E2%80%9CIt%20is%20very%20common%2C%E2%80%9D,have%20unintended%2C%20negative%20consequences.%E2%80%9D&text=%E2%80%9CEveryone%20is%20distracted%2C%E2%80%9D%20Rosenstein,%E2%80%9CAll%20of%20the%20time.%E2%80%9D.
[3] Linda Stone, "Beyond Simple Multi-Tasking: Continuous Partial Attention, Linda Stone Blog, accessed August 31, 2020, https://lindastone.net/2009/11/30/beyond-simple-multi-tasking-continuous-partial-attention/.
[4] Gabe Lyons, "Faithfulness in an Age of Distraction," Q Talks, accessed September 2, 2020, https://media.qideas.org/folder/3b8ac3fa-0b29-4d37-b5ff-5d08b991528d/video/5370fb09-05f7-4038-9d95-6bf0cf2fd084.
[5] Kyle Pearce, "2020 Factsheet on Smartphone Addiction Facts and

Statistics," DIY Genius, February 25, 2020, accessed September 2, 2020. https://www.diygenius.com/smartphone-addiction-factsheet/.
[6] Herbert Simon, "Designing Organizations for an Information-Rich World," ed. Martin Greenberger, *Computers, Communications, and the Public Interest* (Baltimore, MD: Johns Hopkin Press, 1971), 37-52.
[7] Siri Carpenter, "Sights Unseen," American Psychological Association, April 2001, accessed December 10, 2015, http://www.apa.org/monitor/apr01/blindness.aspx.
[8] Nancy K. Napier, "The Myth of Multitasking," *Psychology Today*, May 12, 2014, accessed August 31, 2020, https://www.psychologytoday.com/us/blog/creativity-without-borders/201405/the-myth-multitasking.
[9]John Medina, "The Brain Cannot Multitask," *Brain Rules Blog*, March 16, 2008, accessed December 8, 2015, http://brainrules.blogspot.com/2008/03/brain-cannot-multitask_16.html.
[10] Ibid.
[11] Paul Lewis, "'Our Minds Can Be Hijacked': The Tech Insiders Who Fear A Smartphone Dystopia," *The Guardian*, October 6, 2017, accessed May 1, 2020, https://www.theguardian.com/technology /2017/oct/05/smartphone-addiction-silicon-valley-dystopia.
[12] Ibid.
[13] Ibid.
[14] "Distraction," Merriam-Webster, accessed August 31, 2020, https://www.merriam-webster.com/dictionary/distract#etymology.
[15] O. Alan Noble, "How to Witness to a Distracted World," *Christianity Today*, July 17, 2018, accessed May 3, 2020, https://www.christianitytoday.com/ct/2018/july-web-only/how-to-witness-to-distracted-world-disruptive-witness-noble.html.
[16] "Distraction," Dictionary.com, accessed August 31, 2020, https://www.dictionary.com/browse/distraction?s=t.
[17] Joe Kraus, "We're Creating a Culture of Distraction," *Joe Kraus Blog*, May 25, 2012, accessed December 14, 2015, http://joekraus.com/were-creating-a-culture-of-distraction.
[18] Andrew Sullivan, "I Used to Be a Human Being," *New York Magazine*, September 19, 2016, accessed December 20, 2016, http://nymag.com/selectall/2016/09/andrew-sullivan-technology-almost-killed-me.html.
[19] Sullivan, "I Used to Be a Human Being."
[20] Jenna Perrine, "Creating a Practice-Based Gathering," The Eternal Current Podcast, Episode 6, Part 2, https://podbay.fm/podcast/1476002283/e/1567706652. I have

elaborated to a great extent on Jenna's general premise.
[21] Elizabeth Gilbert, *Eat, Love, Pray: One Woman's Search for Everything Across Italy, India and Indonesia* (New York: Penguin, 2016), 146.
[22] Lucy Shaw, "A Conversation with Eugene Peterson," *Image Journal*, issue 62, accessed August 27, 2020, http://www.imagejournal.org/article/conversation-eugene-peterson/.
[23] Ibid.
[24] Albert Mohler, "The Challenge of Attention in the Digital Age," *Albert Mohler Blog*, May 22, 2008, accessed December 16, 2016, http://www.albertmohler.com/2008/05/22/the-challenge-of-attention-in-the-digital-age/.
[25] Barry D. Jones, *Dwell: Life with God for the World* (Downers Grove, IL: InterVarsity, 2014), 106.
[26] Ibid., 178.

Chapter 5

[1] Sweet, 54.
[2] Mary Oliver, "Attention is the Beginning of Devotion," *The Atlantic,* May 9, 2019, accessed August 31, 2020, https://www.theatlantic.com/technology/archive/2019/05/mary-olivers-poetry-captures-our-relationship-technology/589039/.
[3] M. Craig Barnes, *An Extravagant Mercy* (Ann Arbor, MI: Servant Publications, 2003), 8.
[4] James K.A. Smith, *You Are What You Love: The Spiritual Power of Habit* (Grand Rapids, MI: Baker Publishing Group, 2016), 21.
[5] Ibid., 25.
[6] Oliver, "Attention is the Beginning of Devotion."
[7] Rob Moll, *What Your Body Knows About God: How We Are Designed to Connect, Serve and Thrive* (Downers Grove, IL: InterVarsity Press, 2014), 157.
[8] Diane J. Chandler, *Christian Spiritual Formation: An Integrated Approach for Personal and Relational Wholeness* (Downers Grove, IL: InterVarsity Academics, 2014), 170.
[9] Khaled Hosseini, *The Kite Runner* (Penguin Group: New York, NY, 2003), 359.
[10] Thomas Merton, *Thoughts in Solitude* (New York: Farrar, Straus, and Giroux, 1956), 37.

Chapter 6

---

[1] Howard-John Wesley as quoted by Leonard Blair, "Megachurch Pastor Steps away from Pulpit Because He Feels far from God, Tired in Soul," *Christian Post*, December 11, 2019, accessed April 26, 2020, https://www.christianpost.com/news/megachurch-pastor-steps-away-from-pulpit-because-he-feels-far-from-god-tired-in-soul.html?fbclid=IwAR3I-IlpCJ96BvKau8seZDgDB8YOzThKEIIDd2c98MlrFI8OH2P7aD3vWOw.

[2] Interview with Robert Crosby, *Influence Magazine*, issue 26, November/December 2019, 10-12.

[3] Richard L. Dresselhaus, "Three Miles from the Coffee: A Study in Intimacy with God," *Enrichment Journal*, accessed May 2, 2016, http://enrichmentjournal.ag.org/200403/200403_034_intimacywithGod.cfm.

[4] Ibid.

[5] Ibid.

[6] Leonardo Blair, "Megachurch Pastor Steps away from Pulpit Because He Feels far from God, Tired in Soul," *Christian Post*, December 11, 2019, accessed April 26, 2020, https://www.christianpost.com/news/megachurch-pastor-steps-away-from-pulpit-because-he-feels-far-from-god-tired-in-soul.html?fbclid=IwAR3I-IlpCJ96BvKau8seZDgDB8YOzThKEIIDd2c98MlrFI8OH2P7aD3vWOw.

[7] Kate Shellnut, "Acts 29 CEO Removed Amid Accusations of Abusive Leadership," *Christianity Today*, February 7, 2020, accessed April 26, 2020, https://www.christianitytoday.com/news/2020/february/acts-29-ceo-steve-timmis-removed-spiritual-abuse-tch.html?utm_source=ctweekly-html&utm_medium=Newsletter&utm_term=20178736&utm_content=696075285&utm_campaign=email.

[8] Bob Smietana, "Bill Hybels Resigns from Willow Creek," Christianity Today, April 10, 2018, accessed April 26, 2020, https://www.christianitytoday.com/news/2018/april/bill-hybels-resigns-willow-creek-misconduct-allegations.html

[9] Kate Shellnut. "On Easter Megachurch Backs Pastor Indicted for 3.5 Million Fraud," *Christianity Today*, April 2, 2018, accessed April 26, 2020, https://www.christianitytoday.com/news/2018/april/houston-pastor-kirbyjon-caldwell-indicted-sec-fraud-bonds.html.

[10] Art Toalston, "Southern Baptist Leader Frank Page Resigns over 'Morally Inappropriate Relationship,'" *Christianity Today*, March 27, 2018, accessed April, 26, 2020, https://www.christianitytoday.com/news/2018/march/frank-page-

resigns-southern-baptist-executive-committee-sbc.html.
[11] Anugrah Kumar, "Former So. Baptist Pastor Darrin Patrick Dies of 'Self-Inflicted Gunshot Wound' at 49," *Christian Post*, May 8, 2020, https://www.christianpost.com/news/former-sothern-baptist-pastor-darrin-patrick-dies-by-apparent-suicide-at-49.html.
[12] David Henry Thoreau, *Walden and Civil Disobedience* (Berkeley, CA: Mint Editions, 2020), 10.
[13] Josh Skjoldal, "A Road Out of Wilderness," *Influence Magazine*, issue 19, September/October 2018, 52-59.
[14] Dresselhaus, "Three Miles from the Coffee."
[15] John Ortberg, "The Barnacles of Life," *Christianity Today*, accessed June 2, 2020, https://www.christianitytoday.com/pastors /2015/winter/barnacles-of-life.html.
[16] Blue Letter Bible, "G3306—*meno*—Strong's Greek Lexicon (KJV)," accessed June 5, 2020, https://www.blueletterbible.org/lang/ lexicon/lexicon.cfm?Strongs=G3306&t=KJV.
[17] See John 14:16-17; Romans 8:15-16; Galatians 5:16; Ephesians 3:16-19; 5:18.
[18] See Mark 1:17; 3:14; John 15; 17:3; Galatians 4:9; Colossians 3:1-17.

Chapter 7

[1] Wright, *Mission of God*, 534.
[2] Dallas Willard, "Residency Notes," Spring Arbor University, January 11, 2008.
[3] Blue Letter Bible, "G4160—*Poieō*—Strong's Hebrew Lexicon (NIV), accessed August 31, 2020, https://www.blue letterbible.org/lang/lexicon/lexicon.cfm?Strongs=G4160&t=NIV.
[4] Sweet, *Nudge*, 52.
[5] Andrew Root, *The Pastor in a Secular Age* (Grand Rapids, MI: Baker Academic, 2019), 274.
[6] Praying without ceasing is a persistent New Testament theme. See Matthew 7:7-8; Luke 11:5-13; 18:1; Ephesians 6:18; Colossians 4:2; 1 Thessalonians 1:2; 5:16-18.
[7] Shane Claiborne, Jonathan Wilson-Hartgrove, and Enuma Okoro, *Common Prayer: A Liturgy for Ordinary Radicals* (Grand Rapids, MI: Zondervan, 2010). This prayer is recorded in all of the daily devotions.
[8] Root, *The Pastor in a Secular Age*, 275.
[9] Eugene Peterson, *The Pastor: A Memoir* (New York: HarperCollins, 2011), 142.

Chapter 8

---

[1] Barbara Brown Taylor, *An Altar in the World* (New York: HarperCollins, 2009), 133

[2] Mike Yaconelli, "Clearings," *The Door*, January/February, 1995.

[3] Taylor, *An Altar in the World*, 133.

[4] Ruth Haley Barton, *Silence and Solitude: Experiencing God's Transforming Presence* (Downers Grove, IL: InterVarsity, 2010), 39.

[5] Nick Ross, "In the Shadow of VUCA: A Call for Soul and Sanctuary in Leadership," *Nick Ross LinkedIn Blog*, May 11, 2016, accessed December 18, 2016, https://www.linkedin.com/pulse/shadow-vuca-call-soul-sanctuary-leadership-nick-ross.

[6] Mark Batterson, *If: Trading Your If Only Regrets for God's What If Possibilities* (Grand Rapids, MI: Baker, 2015), 141.

[7] Eugene Peterson, "The Pastor's Sabbath," *Christianity Today*, accessed August 29, 2020, https://www.christianitytoday.com/pastors/leadership-books/prayerpersonalgrowth/lclead04-2.html.

[8] Wayne Muller, *Sabbath: Restoring the Sacred Rhythm of Rest* (New York: Bantam Books, 1999), 1.

[9] Dan Allender, *Sabbath: The Ancient Practices* (Nashville, TN: Thomas Nelson, 2009), 37.

[10] This is in keeping with Deuteronomy 5:12-15.

[11] Unfortunately, I did not record the bibliographic information of the textbook, but the quote occurred on page 310.

[12] Wayne Muller, *Sabbath: Finding Rest, Renewal, and Delight in Our Busy Lives* (Wayne Muller, 1999), 82.

[13] Mark Buchanan, *The Rest of God: Restoring Your Soul by Restoring Sabbath* (Nashville, TN: Thomas Nelson, 2006), 189.

[14] Andy Crouch, *The Tech-Wise Family* (Grand Rapids, MI: Baker Books, 2017), 98.

[15] This 'saying' is similar to Carey Nieuwhof's article title, "If You Don't Take the Sabbath, the Sabbath Will Take You," Carey Nieuwhof, accessed September 18, 2020, https://careynieuwhof.com/if-you-dont-take-the-sabbath-the-sabbath-will-take-you/.

Chapter 9

[1] Nick Ross, "Epoch of Transformation: An Interpersonal Leadership Model for the 21st Century," *Nick Ross blog*, February 25, 2015, accessed June 4, 2020, http://integralleadershipreview.com/6294-epoch-of-transformation-an-interpersonal-leadership-model-for-the-21st-century-part-1/.

[2] Ruth Haley Barton, *Strengthening the Soul of Your Leadership: Seeking God in the Crucible of Ministry* (Downers Grove, IL: InterVarsity, 2008), 23.

---

[3] Seth Richardson. "The Most Important Pastoral Practice of Our Time," *Missio Alliance Blog*, accessed May 22, 2020, https://www.missioalliance.org/important-pastoral-practice-time/.
[4] Collin Hansen, "The Toll of Our Toiling," *Christianity Today*, March 2010, accessed May 22, 2020, https://www.christianitytoday.com/ct/2010/marchweb-only/23-21.0.html.
[5] John Piper, *Brothers, We Are Not Professionals: A Plea to Pastor for Radical Ministry* (Nashville, TN: B&H Publishing Group, 2013), 145.
[6] Todd Wilson, "How Can So Many Pastors Be Godly and Dysfunctional at the Same Time?" *Christianity Today*, July/August 2019, https://www.christianitytoday.com/pastors/2019/spring/integrated-pastor.html.
[7] Thomas Merton, *Thomas Merton: Spiritual Master: The Essential Writings,* ed. with an Introduction by Lawrence S. Cunningham (Foreword by Patrick Hart and Preface by Anne E. Carr) (Mahwah, NJ: Paulist Press: 1992), 375.
[8] Stephen I. Woodworth, "Why Do Some Pastor Sabotage Their Ministry?" *Christianity Today*, April 2020, accessed June 6, 2020, https://www.christianitytoday.com/pastors/2019/june-web-exclusives/why-do-some-pastors-sabotage-their-own-ministries.html?utm_source=ctweekly-html&utm_medium=Newsletter&utm_term=20178736&utm_content=654655494&utm_campaign=email.
[9] Ross, "In the Shadow."
[10] Brene Brown, *The Gifts of Imperfection: Let Go of Wo You Think You Are Supposed to Be and Embrace Who You Are* (Center City, MN: Hazelden, 2010), 23.
[11] David Letterman, *Parade Magazine*, May 26, 1996, 6.
[12] "Jim Carrey Speech at The Golden Globe Awards 2016 HDTV," January 12, 2016, YouTube, accessed August 29, 2020, https://www.youtube.com/watch?v=a9J8GaeDqVc.
[13] Brene Brown, "The Power of Vulnerability," TED Talk, accessed September 1, 2020, https://www.ted.com/talks/brene_brown_the_power_of_vulnerability?language=en.
[14] Dan Allender and Tremper Longman, *The Cry of the Soul* (Colorado Springs, CO: NavPress, 1994), 24.
[15] Hillsong Worship, "Glorious Ruins," Worship Together, accessed August 29, 2020, https://www.worshiptogether.com/songs/glorious-ruins-hillsong-worship/.

Chapter 10

[1] Dan White, Jr., quoted by Angela Craig, "Broken Perfectionism," Journey Online, accessed August 29, 2020, https://journeyonline.org/broken-perfectionism/.
[2] Michael Thompson. *The Congruent Life: Following the inward Path to Fulfilling Work and Inspired Leadership* (San Francisco: Jossey-Bass Publishers, 2000), 150.
[3] Tad Dunne, *Spiritual Mentoring: Guiding People through Spiritual Exercises to Life Decision* (New York: Harper Collins, 1991), 84.
[4] John Baillie, *A Diary of Private Prayer* (New York: Fireside, 1949), 27.
[5] Smith, *You Are What You Love*, 52.
[6] Marjorie Thompson, *Soul Feast: An Invitation to the Christian Spiritual Life* (Louisville, KY: Westminster John Knox Press, 2005), 90.
[7] Daniel J. Siegel, *Mindsight: The New Science of Personal Transformation* (New York: Bantam Books, 2010), 211.
[8] Shelly Trebesch, *Isolation: A Place of Transformation in the Life of a Leader* (Altadena CA: Barnabas Publishers, 1997), 56.
[9] Chuck DeGroat, *Wholeheartedness: Busyness, Exhaustion, and Healing the Divided Self* (Grand Rapids, MI: Eerdmans, 2016), 151.
[10] K. J. Ramsey, "There's No Shame When a Miracle Doesn't Come," *Christianity Today*, December 27, 2019, accessed June 2, 2020, https://www.christianitytoday.com/ct/2019/december-web-only/wakeupolive-heiligenthal-bethel-church-miracle-doesnt-come.html?utm_source=outreach-html&utm_medium=Newsletter&utm_term=23350038&utm_content=695728386&utm_campaign=email.
[11] Lissa Rankin, "The Healing Power of Telling Your Story," *Psychology Today*, November 27, 2012, accessed April 26, 2020, https://www.psychologytoday.com/blog/owning-pink/201211/the-healing-power-telling-your-story.
[12] Daniel Goleman, "The Focused Leader," *Harvard Business Review*, December 2013, accessed April 24, 2020, https://hbr.org/2013/12/the-focused-leader.
[13] Keith Anderson, *A Spirituality of Listening: Living What We Hear* (Downers Grove, IL: InterVarsity, 2016), 83.
[14] Blue Letter Bible, "G1843—*exomologeō*—Strong's Hebrew Lexicon (NIV), accessed August 31, 2020, https://www.blueletterbible.org/lang/lexicon/lexicon.cfm?Strongs=G1843&t=NIV.

---

[15] Blue Letter Bible, "G266—*hamartia*—Strong's Hebrew Lexicon (NIV), accessed August 31, 2020, https://www.blueletterbible.org/lang/lexicon/lexicon.cfm?Strongs=G266&t=NIV.
[16] Brennan Manning, *Abba's Child: The Cry of the Heart for Intimate Belonging* (Colorado Spring, CO: NavPress, 2015), 34.
[17] Brene Brown, *Gifts of Imperfection*, xiv.
[18] Anderson, *A Spirituality of Listening*, 133.
[19] Ibid., 132.

Chapter 11

[1] Brennan Manning, *The Furious Longing of God* (Colorado Spring, CO: David C. Cook, 2009), 75.
[2] Root, *The Pastor in a Secular Age*, 31.
[3] Barna, "The Trends Shaping a Post-Truth Society," Barna, accessed June 2, 2020, https://www.barna.com/research/truth-post-truth-society/.
[4] Root, *The Pastor in a Secular Age*, 195.
[5] Joe Castleberry, Northwest University, President's Blog, accessed June 10, 2020, https://www.northwestu.edu/president/blog/leading-by-ear/?utm_source=Mark+TEST&utm_campaign=6b1ead5eff-EMAIL_CAMPAIGN_2019_01_10_08_57_COPY_01&utm_medium=email&utm_term=0_3383955b60-6b1ead5eff-.
[6] Joshua D. Chatraw, *Telling a Better Story: How to Talk About God in a Skeptical Age* (Grand Rapids, MI: Zondervan, 2020), 8.
[7] Belden Lane, *The Solace of Fierce Landscapes* (New York: Oxford University Press, 1998), 189.
[8] Michael Frost, *Excarnate: The Body of Christ in an Age of Disenchantment* (Downers Grove, IL: InterVarsity, 2014), 168.

Chapter 12

[1] David Augsburger, *Caring Enough to Hear and Be Heard* (Ventura, CA: Regal, 1982), 12.
[2] Adam McHugh, *The Listening Life: Embracing Attentiveness in a World of Distraction* (Downers Grove, IL: InterVarsity, 2015), 143.
[3] Parker Palmer, "The Gift of Presence, The Peril of Advice," On Being Blog, April 27, 2016, accessed April 28, 2017, https://onbeing.org/blog/the-gift-of-presence-the-perils-of-advice/.
[4] Henri J.M. Nouwen, *Reaching Out: The Three Movements of the Spiritual Life* (New York: Doubleday, 1975), 51.
[5] Root, *The Pastor in a Secular Age*, 209.
[6] Sweet, *Nudge*, 105.

[7] Earl Creps, "Disciplemaking in a Postmodern World," *Enrichment Journal* 7, no. 4 (Fall 2002): 52-59.

Acknowledgments

Projects of this sort are never a solo endeavor. This book was birthed from my own journey of leadership over a lifetime of ministry. Thus, this project reflects the contribution of many people in so many different ways.

There is always a danger in calling out specific individuals because inevitably you leave someone out. I would be amiss, however, not to do so.

Thank you, Darrel, for never complaining about the long hours I spent in my office. Your belief in me has changed my life. Thank you for being my biggest supporter. Most of all, thank you for out-loving my brokenness and giving me space and grace to live into God's creative will in my life.

Dr. James Bradford, our happenstance meeting turned into a God-orchestrated friendship. Thank you for your gracious encourage-ment and thoughtful words.

Sue Nelson, it was a delight to drink from your deep well. Your thoughtful insights were always a treasure.

Dr. Jodi Detrick, my iron-sharpening, coaching friend who asked the question who started it all.

Lindsey Jelmberg, you brought lightness to my words and smiles in the margins.

Dr. Robert Woods, your passion to help struggling writers (like me) was such a gift! Your communication skills and expertise were invaluable. This book would be different without you.

Dr. Rosemarie Kowalski, nothing got past your keen editing eye. You made me a better writer. You were kind in your corrections and generous in your encouragement.

Dr. Kim Martinez, I love that we think so differently! My book is richer because of you. Your enthusiasm kept me going when I wanted to quit.

Dr. Lois Olena, for guiding such a careful editing process. Thank you for your patience with all my editing changes!

Brent Johnsen, I don't know many people who are so incredibly intellectual and yet equally abounding with humor as you are. I am grateful for your eyes on this.

Devyn North, your professional graphic skills made my book standout and be noticed!

To those leaders who allowed me the privilege of accompanying them on their spiritual journey of keeping company with Jesus, I offer deep gratitude. Thank you for your honesty, vulnerability, courage, and trusting me with such a treasure.

I thank all the people who read parts of this book, offered comments, and words of encouragement.

To those who listened to my endless requests for prayer … and prayed … for so long. Your patience and gentle inquiries into progress meant so much to me.

May this book accomplish all that God put in my heart for it to accomplish for His glory.

Made in the USA
Coppell, TX
04 August 2022